UNFUCK YOUR SHAME

Dr. Faith G. Harper, ACS, ACN

UNFUCK YOUR SHAME

Using Science to Accept Our Feelings, Resolve Guilt, and Connect with Ourselves

Dr. Faith G. Harper, ACS, ACN

Microcosm Publishing

Portland, Ore | Cleveland, Ohio

UNFUCK YOUR SHAME: Using Science to Accept Our Feelings, Resolve Guilt, and Connect with Ourselves

© Dr. Faith G. Harper, 2024

First edition - 5,000 copies - July 30, 2024

ISBN 9781648413896

This is Microcosm #852

Edited by Kandi Zeller
Cover and design by Joe Biel
This edition © Microcosm Publishing, 2024
For a catalog, write or visit:
Microcosm Publishing
2752 N Williams Ave.
Portland, OR 97227

All the news that's fit to print at www.Microcosm.Pub/Newsletter.

Get more copies of this book at **www.Microcosm.Pub/Shame**
Find more work by Dr. Faith at **www.Microcosm.Pub/DrFaith**

To join the ranks of high-class stores that feature Microcosm titles, talk to your rep: In the U.S. **COMO** (Atlantic), **ABRAHAM** (Midwest), **BOB BARNETT** (Texas, Oklahoma, Arkansas, Louisiana), **IMPRINT** (Pacific), **TURNAROUND** (UK), **UTP/MANDA** (Canada), **NEWSOUTH** (Australia/New Zealand), **Observatoire** (Africa, Europe), **IPR** (Middle East), **Yvonne Chau** (Southeast Asia), **HarperCollins** (India), **Everest/B.K. Agency** (China), **Tim Burland** (Japan/Korea), and **FAIRE** and **EMERALD** in the gift trade.

Did you know that you can buy our books directly from us at sliding scale rates? Support a small, independent publisher and pay less than Amazon's price at **www.Microcosm.Pub**.

Global labor conditions are bad, and our roots in industrial Cleveland in the '70s and '80s made us appreciate the need to treat workers right. Therefore, our books are MADE IN THE USA.

Library of Congress Cataloging-in-Publication Data
    Names: Harper, Faith G., author.
    Title: Unfuck your shame : using science to accept our feelings, resolve guilt, and connect with ourselves / Faith G. Harper, PhD.
    Description: [Portland] : Microcosm Publishing, [2024] | Summary: "Shame and guilt are perhaps the most difficult emotions humans experience. They tell us we are fundamentally broken, wrong, and unsalvageable—and then we operate in the world from that self-concept. Dr. Faith G. Harper, bestselling author of Unfuck Your Brain and Unfuck Your Stress, writes that these emotions often result from our sense of "not-enough-ness" and the overwhelming feeling that we need to hide parts of ourselves in order to be loved and accepted. But we don't need to keep going through life feeling guilty, ashamed, and disconnected from ourselves"-- Provided by publisher.
    Identifiers: LCCN 2023050202 | ISBN 9781648413896 (trade paperback)
    Subjects: LCSH: Shame. | Self-actualization (Psychology)
    Classification: LCC BF575.S45 H37 2024 | DDC 152.4/4--dc23/eng/20231116
    LC record available at https://lccn.loc.gov/2023050202

MICROCOSM · PUBLISHING

Microcosm Publishing is Portland's most diversified publishing house and distributor, with a focus on the colorful, authentic, and empowering. Our books and zines have put your power in your hands since 1996, equipping readers to make positive changes in their lives and in the world around them. Microcosm emphasizes skill-building, showing hidden histories, and fostering creativity through challenging conventional publishing wisdom with books and bookettes about DIY skills, food, bicycling, gender, self-care, and social justice. What was once a distro and record label started by Joe Biel in a drafty bedroom was determined to be *Publishers Weekly*'s fastest-growing publisher of 2022 and #3 in 2023 and 2024, and is now among the oldest independent publishing houses in Portland, OR, and Cleveland, OH. We are a politically moderate, centrist publisher in a world that has inched to the right for the past 80 years.

TABLE OF CONTENTS

INTRODUCTION

I never write the introduction first. Generally, I have to go back and realize everything I ended up writing about so I can write a proper one. But this time, I actually am writing the intro first because I know exactly how this book is going to lay out and I'm super excited for you to hang out with me. The focus of this book is on the science of shame as an emotional state and how to create your own path of healing.

Now, I'm presuming that you are reading (or listening) to this book on purpose. There may be a couple of you staying in an AirBnB somewhere and this was on the shelf and you couldn't sleep and were bored. No worries, glad to have you here! But for the rest of us? We are looking to figure out some bullshit going on in our lives that is causing constant, shitty, exhausting issues.

You have probably read a lot regarding shame, tried some interesting stuff, gotten some new insights and support . . . but found no real healing.

This feel accurate to your experience? Mine too.

We've been frustrated as fuck . . . and maybe getting pushback—from treatment providers and loved ones—of the following ilk:

- "You aren't really trying to get better."

- "Are you even taking your meds?"

- "Ok, but this treatment works for everyone. I don't understand why you're struggling."

- "Are you enjoying playing the victim? Don't you want to get better?"

- "Have you tried green tea and yoga?"

And no shade to green tea and yoga. I'm a 500-hour trained yoga instructor who happens to love jasmine green tea. But it doesn't solve the shame problem. Neither does continuing to shame people struggling to get better: so none of that is happening here, pinky swear.

And here's the thing: many Western medicine approaches aren't effective at treating shame in everyone. But that doesn't mean we are going to be randomly woo-woo. We're gonna be research-backed woo-woo, instead.

This is also not going to be a repeat of any Brené Brown book. She's ubiquitous, so you've either read her already or don't wanna. I gotta throw her name out there right away, because praise be Dr. Brown for bringing the concept of shame more thoroughly into our cultural discourse. Her work in the field has been of value. But it isn't near all of what's out there.

I'm known for leaning hard into brain science in my books, and I'm going to do the same here. And that led me to recognize that much of our cultural discourse *around* the experience of shame doesn't include some incredibly helpful research that wasn't much noticed outside academic circles. About how shame works physiologically in the body, and how different it is from other emotions considered similar. Because hella important.

But also about how trauma and treatment-resistant forms of other mental health issues like depression connect to shame—also really fucking important.

Basically, we're going to be talking about things that changed my clinical work around shame. Because they helped my clients feel seen, heard, and validated in critical ways. And created a new (but actually ancient) pathway to healing.

Because I'm gonna get weird on that part. You know how sometimes you gotta fix shit old-school style? We're going to fix shit *very* old-school style. As in ancient times. Because just because a healing method has been considered primitive doesn't mean it doesn't fucking WORK. Because many ancient methods do, in fact, work. We are seeing "modern" medicine return to our healing roots, using our new ways of measuring treatment success. *And we are finding treatment success.* So our focus in this book is on the methods related to shadow work and soul retrieval.

So please hang with me. I might just convince you I'm on to something here.

But first of all, let's throw in a little breathing exercise. A simple one, designed for grounding, in case any of the work in this book feels like a lot to you. You can go back and use this breathing technique at any time.

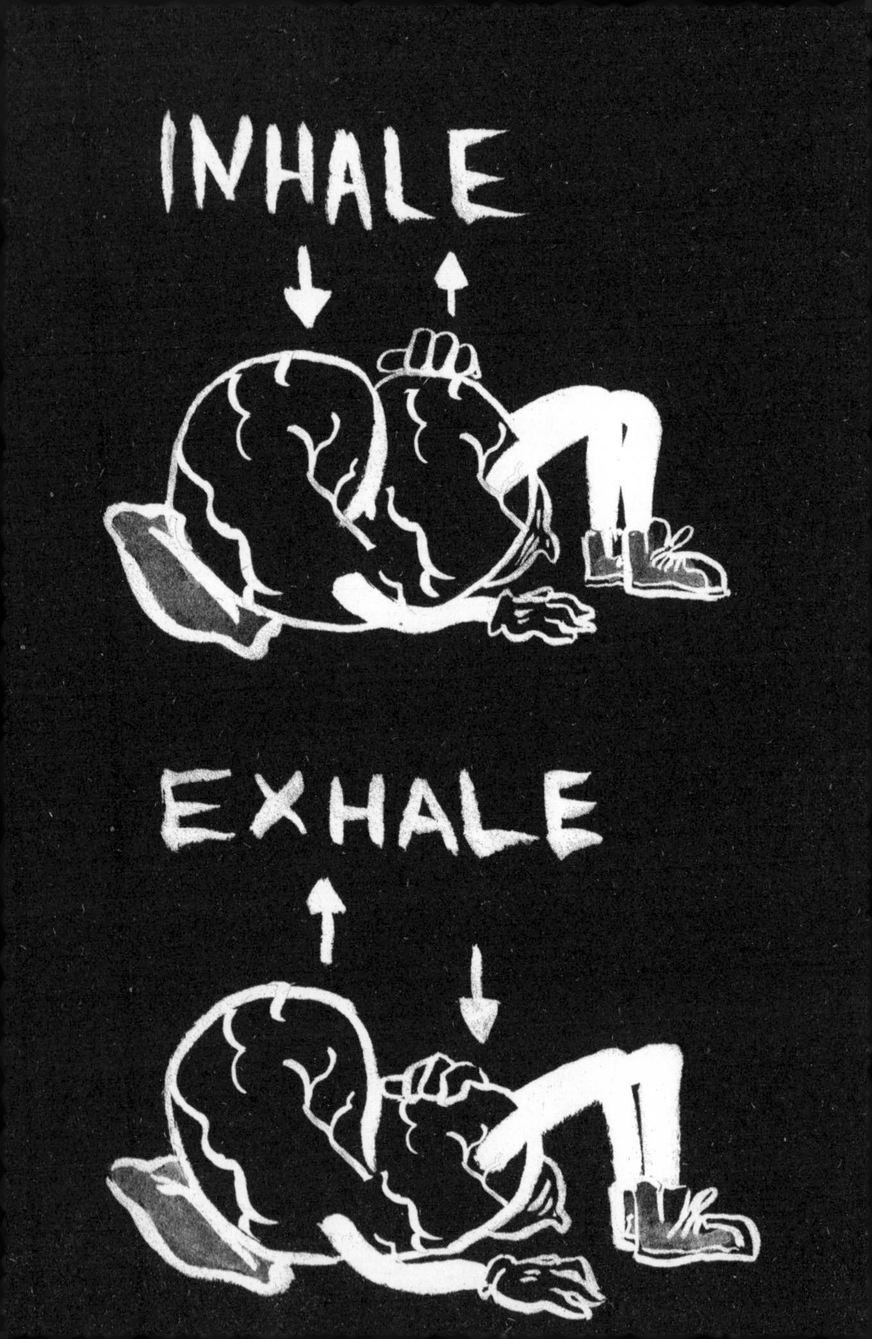
INHALE
EXHALE

SQUARE BREATHING

*T*his breathing tool is simple to use and also isn't consciousness-altering, while still having lots of research behind its benefits in managing anxiety, stress, and activation. So if other breathwork exercises tended to do the opposite of what people told you they would do? And you felt spacey and out of it, instead of relaxed? This one may work better. Along with this technique, you can also use the diaphragmatic breathing technique in the soul retrieval section of this book on page 125 for a similar effect. (This one is just slightly easier and less likely to make you feel too altered.)

And, if you are reading a paper copy of the book, you can even use the printed square as something to trace with your finger while trying the exercise.

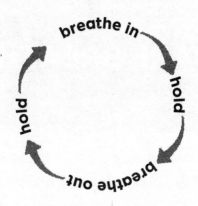

Square-breathing diagram

Start by just paying attention to your breathing for about a minute, and see what you notice by being mindful, without actively trying to change your breathing patterns. Are they rapid? Shallow? Are you holding your breath?

Now, try the following for at least another minute:

1. Breathe in, through your nose, counting to four slowly. Focus on feeling the air enter your lungs. You can trace the top of the box diagram from left to right to help guide you.

2. Hold your breath for another four seconds, trying—if your lung capacity allows you—to not

inhale or exhale during that time period. To help guide you, you can trace down the right side of the bottom of the box diagram from the top point you landed on.

3. Now, slowly exhale through your mouth for another four seconds. You can trace across the bottom of the box, now going right to left, if that helps guide you.

4. Hold your breath again for another four seconds.

Repeat this exercise as many times as you can. Even thirty seconds of deep breathing will help you feel more relaxed and in control.

Part 1: What Is Shame?

*S*imply put, shame is a belief that you are bad and nothing can be done about it. It's a response to any feedback that tells us our personhood is fundamentally wrong and broken.

To get a better handle on how shame works, we're going to turn to some more complex and "official" definitions, as well as some fascinating brain research around shame.

According to the Oxford English Dictionary, shame is . . .

> the painful emotion arising from the consciousness of something dishonoring, ridiculous or indecorous in one's own conduct or circumstances (or in those of others whose honor or disgrace one regards as one's own), or of being in a situation which offends one's sense of modesty or decency (OED online, December 2014).

More specifically, shame is a self-conscious emotion, because it exists only within our evaluation of ourselves. It's also considered an incapacitating emotion, because we quite literally shrink our psyche in the face of believing we are not enough, no good, and not deserving of care and consideration. Shame tells us we are incompetent and inadequate. Inferior. Worthless.

Interestingly, researchers don't think that shame is a core emotion we are born with, like joy, anger, and sadness. Shame, by contrast, is an emotion of self-consciousness. Like pride, embarrassment, empathy, envy, and guilt, shame depends on specific cognitive developments around self-awareness. In other words, once we know we exist—as in, we can look in a mirror and go "Oh shit . . . it me!"—we can experience self-evaluation. Meaning, "It me . . . and I like me!" or "It me . . . and, gross, who let me out into the world?" . . . and all evaluations in between. This starts to kick in between 18 and 24 months of age. And once we develop self-representations, we can recognize external rules and values from the world around us and then evaluate ourselves based on these newly-formed cultural expectations.

But shame doesn't just stay in our thoughts. It has a behavioral component to it as well, but not a universal one.

This is kinda (read: really) interesting. Core emotions tend to look the same across humanity. We know what a mad face looks like on any continent of the world, right? (Paul Ekman—who the TV show Lie to Me was based on—spent a brilliant career studying these universal expressions.)

But because shame is an emotion of self-appraisal in which we find ourselves lacking, shame activates our stress response, and we respond with defense. This phenomenon is what psychiatrist Donald Nathanson developed a model for in 1992, to explain the different ways we cope with shame.

• *isolating oneself*
• *running and hiding*

"turning the tables"
blaming the victim
lashing out verbally or physically

self put-down
masochism

WITHDRAWAL

ATTACK OTHER

ATTACK SELF

AVOIDANCE

• *denial*
• *abusing drugs and alcohol*
• *distraction through thrill-seeking*

Adapted depiction of Donald Nathanson's Compass of Shame, with compass points for withdrawal, attack self, avoidance, and attack other.

Withdrawal is what happens when we determine the shame we are experiencing is well-deserved—leading us to want to minimize our exposure to others. This can look like a lot of things: a movement away from connection, self-isolation (either physically or emotionally), and other mechanisms for removing ourselves in one way or another. (Nathanson noted that withdrawal as a shame response is likely a form of atypical depression, especially when it's a prolonged experience and comes with fear of being "in trouble" for your wrongness. We're going to talk about shame and depression and dissociation in much more detail later in the book, so just note this phenomenon for right now.)

Attack Self refers to another way of immediately owning the shame experience as deserved and valid. However instead of withdrawing, individuals who attack self want to maintain connection with others. So they self-criticize and act with deference to those around them, in order to better conform to the ideal self others expect from them. They're like a beaten animal that gets kicked and comes back, then licks the hand of the person who kicked them.

Avoidance, unlike withdrawal, is when people work to deny the shame message at some level. So they avoid any situations or people who activated the feeling in the first place. They are also far more likely to use things—like alcohol, drugs, and thrill-seeking behaviors—that let them avoid their feeling state. Nathanson noted that avoidance behaviors are the ones that are most buried in the preconscious mind. Meaning that the behaviors don't even register as a shame response to avoidant people.

Attack Other refers to the ways in which we look to boost our own self-esteem at the expense of those around us. Self-esteem is externally created and validated, unlike self-compassion, self-empathy, and self-worth. That isn't a bad thing or a good thing . . . it's just a thing to be aware of when we talk about psychological concepts. Say you study hard for a test. Your self-esteem is fabulous if you nail it . . . and may bottom out if you don't. The results of the test are used to define who you are. So individuals who attack others need to have comparative results that tell them they are better. And that may involve blaming or put downs. At the extreme end, it could also include interpersonal violence.

Nathanson noted that in the US, the dominant cultural models lean more into avoidance and attacking others, especially since the second half of the twentieth century. He was developing his model at the same time the century was ending, so it's a solid observation.

This means if you live outside the US—or even if you live outside the dominant culture within the US—you may notice very different patterns. But wherever you live, it is an interesting point, I think, to look at how powerful shame is. It shapes many negative aspects of our interpersonal relationships to such an extreme that we can see it changing society as a whole. That's a heavy realization, enit?

And if the emotion of shame is that excruciating and important in how it shapes our lives? We should be talking about it way more and way differently. So put on your comfiest science pants, and let's get to it.

THE SCIENCE OF SHAME

*T*here has been a jump in both community and clinical interest in shame in recent years. But one thing surprised me when I dove into the research around shame: Despite this renewed interest, the research in this area has focused more on shame susceptibility, instead of the experience and management of shame. In other words, there's more research about our likelihood to experience shame than there is about what that experience is like and how we can effectively manage it. And this reality is as important as it is confusing, so let's unpack it a little.

Shame *susceptibility* research focuses on the factors that contribute to the type of personality that tends to strongly align with a sense of shame. Meaning, what factors lead us to self-evaluate constantly to the negative? This tendency—to look at what predisposes people to shame—is so common in the discourse around shame research that shame itself is now starting to get conflated as a human *trait* instead of an emotional *state* (by both the research community and larger society). But the difference between traits and states is enormous.

Traits are long-lasting, stable, and internally activated constructs. Meaning . . . traits are who you are, genetically (genes themselves) or epigenetically (the heritable altering of gene expression due to trauma). By contrast, emotional states are brief, temporary, and caused by external circumstances.

And so by conflating the two terms, we are treating shame as something we are, instead of something that we experience because something shitty happened to us.

So most forms of media around shame that you've read/listened to in the past? They are likely focused on state-based trauma; they are about building your self-worth and things that prop up your personhood. Instead of focusing on what happened in your life that activates a shame response.

But shame as an emotional state has been studied in the past, just less recently. That past research itself is incredibly helpful to our cause, though the suggested interventions (as you will see) are far less helpful. But, hey, that research is still a good starting point to get us to where we are trying to go.

Silvan Tomkins (who had a masters in psychology and a PhD in philosophy) developed affect theory back in the 60s, naming our innate biological responses as affects. *Affects* are just any emotion with a biological root. Which is all of them.

This was super cutting edge at the time. Too bad he decided that therapy should only focus on increasing positive emotions and decreasing negative ones. And that Christian religion should be universal because it provides this solution: focus on positive, disregard negative.

Bruh. No.

But based on that work, clinical psychologist and professor Gershen Kaufman posited that this biological motivation for shame—coupled with our competencies, needs, drives, etc.—creates individuals who see themselves continuously as unworthy, inferior people. Kaufman referred to these individuals as having "shame-bound personalities" and "shame-based identities."

Bruh? NO!

Victim blaming (victim shaming?) is never fucking helpful. Any more so than the "y'all need Jesus" argument posited by Tomkins. But the idea that shame is a *socially engineered* emotion created a starting point for research and treatment that we have focused on to this day.

Because, if shame is a socially engineered emotion, it means circumstances around us are activating our shame responses.

In other words, expressions that nod to our personalities or identities being shame-based don't mean shame is a trait. Instead, this points to the fact that people who have complicated lives typically have more frequent experiences which activate the emotional state of shame. Therefore, the dynamics of shame being interpersonal are what we should be attending to.

Socially Engineered Shame

Many theorists over the past decades have provided support to the idea that the emotion of shame results from social interactions; it doesn't exist in and of itself. In order to be ashamed of yourself, you have to be evaluating yourself through the eyes of someone else. Someone with enough power to judge you negatively and have it impact you.

Sociologist Thomas Scheff has been writing about shame as a social emotion since the 1970s, going so far as to define shame as an awareness of relational problems. Which means that shame not only arises from social interactions but also continues to shape them. Additionally, shame is associated with other social self-appraisals, like weakness, worthlessness, and rejection.

And while any of these particular thoughts are incredibly damaging, it gets even more complicated. As we discussed earlier, shame leads to an impulse to hide ourselves from others because we feel fundamentally damaged and broken. We feel like we need to remove ourselves from others. We avoid interactions, sabotage relationships, and dissociate from our own experiences.

At this point, it's important to note that, if shame is a relational emotion, then it is also culture-bound. In countries that are accepting of both shame and the process of working through it, it can be acknowledged and processed. Psychiatrist Kenichiro Okano started writing about how the acknowledgement of shame in Japanese culture allows for everyone to hold up social bonds, unlike in the United States. He noticed that in the US, where we are culturally less forgiving of demonstrations of vulnerability, we won't process our shame experiences directly. Instead, we are more likely to externalize by lashing out with rage or hostility against those we perceive as shaming us.

This theory gave researchers something to test.

Were Okano and Scheff right that the biggest problem shame presents is when its existence is denied or unacknowledged?

Research around shame experiences comparing Japan and the US does lend credence to this theory. So it seems to be true that the damage of shame comes from being ashamed of our shame. We try to escape it by hiding it or blaming others, causing enormous problems in the process, on both relational and cultural levels. And while Tomkins may have had strongly held beliefs that having Jesus in your life would solve your shame, only about 1% of the population of Japan is Chirstian, and they seem to have better processes in place for working through shame as an emotional response, rather than treating it as a personality flaw.

But shame isn't solely a social problem. And, hey? Didn't Tomkins also say affects had biological underpinnings? Shouldn't we look at that, as well?

The Biological Mechanisms

Tomkins was totally right about shame having a physiological process in the body, and it turns out the research around how the body experiences shame is vitally important.

One of the most fascinating aspects of this research is how shame is connected to the emotion of disgust. In neuroimaging, both shame and disgust are associated with the activation of the anterior cingulate cortex (ACC) and the anterior insula. In fact, disgust shows specific activation of the ACC subregion associated with how we process social interactions.

When I first read these studies, it weirded me out. Why are we not talking about this? Shame is, as we went over, a secondary emotion designed to help humans maintain social order through social hierarchy.

But what about disgust? Let's get into that a bit, like the knowledge nerds we are. As an emotion, disgust is designed to prevent disease as part of the behavioral immune system (BIS).

The behavioral immune system is different from our biological immune system. The biological immune system defends the body against pathogens that have already entered. The behavioral immune system encourages us to avoid any situations that could lead to being contaminated by pathogens, and it includes not only emotions of disgust, but also accompanying thoughts ("Ew, is that dirty?") and behaviors (recoiling, avoidance).

Disgust is a strong, visceral reaction, right? Like if you have ever smelled spoiled food and almost barfed just from the smell? Disgust. Your body interprets that scent as DANGEROUS and recoils immediately. Of course, people have different disgust sensitivities, based on life experiences and, quite likely, epigenetic ones. Since there is variance in our disgust experiences (for some people it's really strong, for others it barely exists . . . and most of us fall somewhere between these groups), a person's disgust experience is still considered a personality characteristic rather than a purely physiological response. Just like shame.

SHAME VS. GUILT

So if disgust and shame are related, how do shame and guilt connect? Shame and guilt are similar in many ways, enough so that they are often conflated in our day-to-day communications. But the differences that do exist are really important.

So all that stuff about how shame and disgust both activate a specific region of the ACC known for social information processing? Guilt doesn't do that. Guilt is associated with activation of the dorsomedial prefrontal cortex (PFC) as well as the superior frontal gyrus,[1] supramarginal gyrus, and anterior inferior frontal gyrus.

So while guilt can be anxiety-provoking and *may* activate the amygdala (the part of the brain most

---

[1] Trivia nerd alert: gyri are those bumpy elevated parts of the cerebral cortex.

associated with emotional processes), to some extent, guilt is primarily a PFC activity.

And if you are wondering if guilt has the same disgust component that shame does? Nope, it doesn't. Researchers have invoked disgust and seen what that does to feelings of both guilt and shame, and only shame correlates (even after controlling for negative emotions).

And even though both shame and guilt are prosocial emotions, our brains attribute guilt to a specific circumstance or behavior: meaning it lets us know that we made a mistake and we need to take accountability and correct what we can. In other words, guilt pushes us toward repair.

By contrast, shame, because it activates disgust, tells us to remove ourselves from the situation in question. That we are a contaminant. That the repair in question *is our disappearance.*

So if accountability and repair don't provide relief from shame, what are we supposed to do? Research in Western medicine paradigms don't really have the answer, which you likely remember me being cranky about at the beginning of this book. Later on, we'll get into more detail about how non-Western paradigms open up a path forward to healing. But first, we need to talk a bit more about what we lose to shame and what role trauma plays in the process.

WHAT DO WE LOSE TO SHAME?

*I*f shame is a disease of self-disgust, it can cause us to lose access to our ability to know and meet our own needs. Dr. Cloé Madanes, who trains people in both family therapy and life coaching practices, delineated six fundamental human needs. The first four are fundamental for human survival (needs of the body) and the last two are essential to human fulfillment (needs of the spirit). This list is an excellent starting point to look more deeply at what we may be losing to shame.

So take a look at these six needs and consider how shame has impacted the fulfillment of these needs in your life.

1. **Certainty:** We need safety, stability, and predictability. We want a level of assurance that

our needs will be met and we can avoid pain. But also . . .

2. **Variety:** Too much safety and stability and we get bored and disengaged from life because things are too certain. We need change, excitement, and new stimuli. The people who need the most variety sometimes seek out crisis and conflict to have this need met.

3. **Significance:** We need our lives and work to have meaning and importance.

4. **Connection:** We need affiliation with others, to feel part of a community.

5. **Growth:** We need goals to strive for and challenges to undertake. Human brains need problems to solve that are solvable. We are happiest when we see progress in our goals.

6. **Contribution:** We need to feel we have made a difference and contribute in ways to the greater community.

Now, read these needs in light of shame responses by considering the following questions:

- What have you noticed about patterns in your own life?

- Where has shame removed you from having these needs met?

- Which losses are most obvious?

- Which are more subtle?

- Did anything surprise you upon reflection?

Knowing what shame can take from us, let's look at some important limitations in shame research and how those limitations point us to a possible new path forward in our journeys to heal from shame.

SHAME RESEARCH LIMITATIONS

*D*espite all we know about shame through research, we have continued to focus on shame as a personality trait (the *people* who are more predisposed to experience shame) than an emotion (the *events* that tend to cause shame and how to work through it). Which is kind of a big problem.

Not that dispositional shame—the idea of what factors, such as other mental health issues, might be associated with people who experience shame chronically—is a bad topic to research. It definitely isn't.

Understanding how shame is correlated with other mental health issues *is* important, and I am going to talk about that subject too. But it isn't the only important feature we should be looking at. Nor is it, I would argue, the most important feature of shame in general.

But if the vast majority of the research out there focuses on shame as this intrapsychic[2] process, we aren't really looking at what is going on around us in the world that causes us to experience shame.

If we are recognizing shame as a social emotion, shouldn't we be looking at social factors? If we are in agreement that shame exists in a relational context? You may not agree with me that this is the most important aspect, but I think we are all in agreement that we shouldn't be ignoring social context (meaning *what happens to us*) that exacerbates the emotion of shame.

So, again, dispositional shame research mostly focuses on individuals who tend to experience shame chronically and what other factors may be associated with it, like other psychological problems (such as depression, anxiety) and adverse childhood experiences (traumatic stress). Between 1997 and 2011, there were 43 empirical studies of shame. Only three of these studies really looked at how we respond to naturally occurring instances of shame—how we work with shame, manage shame, and communicate around it. This means all the

---

2 Which just refers to the process that happens within our own minds (psyches).

rest, in some manner, were really about just recognizing, "Lot of shame there, eh? More's the pity!"

When we consider how impactful shame is to all things social—on both interpersonal and cultural levels—that's not a lot of research about the social causes of shame.

When we look at shame only as an embedded state, we're not looking at social factors nearly as much as would be helpful for clinical care. If shame is a relational emotion, the fact that we aren't doing any research on how it emerges in relationships—and can be healed in relationships—is . . . fucked. It's just fucked, y'all. We can't uncouple the experience of shame from the contexts that create it, and we can't heal shame without understanding how it arises in these contexts.

Which means . . . we gotta talk about trauma and trauma responses.

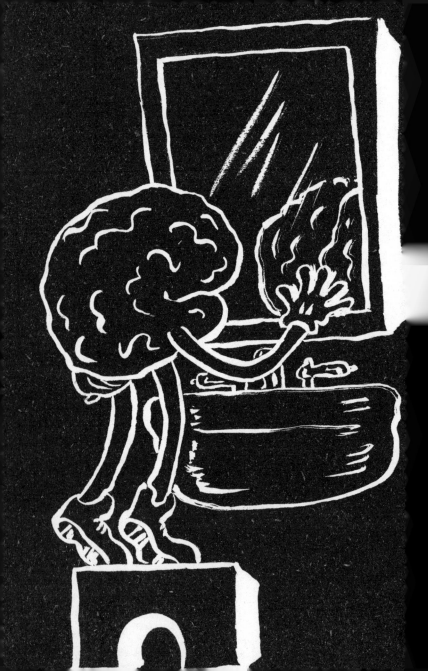

TRAUMA AND ITS EMOTIONAL OUTFALL

I apologize for dragging trauma into every wellness conversation I undertake, but I haven't yet found an emotional health topic that doesn't bump into trauma.

(Also, apparently it's my brand at this point. And . . . this is why I'm not invited to parties.)

And when I took some deeper dives into the research, really looking for more on shame as an emotional state rather than a personality trait, I found . . . trauma research. Specifically, significant research on how shame is activated within individuals with unhealed trauma, who are being misdiagnosed as experiencing depression. And this leads us to more research on what is referred to as dissociative depression.

Dissociation and Dissociative Depression

Dissociation has been very Tik Tok–trendy as of late, which I have mixed feelings about as an Official Old Person. While open public conversations about mental health issues are way-fucking-overdue, social media comes with misinformation, which, in this case, diminishes how serious dissociation really is. For example, when people say they were triggered when they were uncomfortable. Or when many people discussing dissociation in their own lives are actually discussing just being checked out from their surroundings, when the reality of dissociation is far more serious.

We have two manuals from which licensed clinicians can diagnose, and the one most often used in the US is the *Diagnostic and Statistical Manual* published by the American Psychiatric Association. The DSM-V-TR is the current version as of this writing, and defines dissociation as: "disruption of and/or discontinuity in the normal integration of consciousness, memory, identity, emotion, perception, body representation, motor control, and behavior."

All human beings experience this, and not just for vagal tone reasons. Have you ever been super absorbed in something you love doing? A book, a movie, a game, a hobby you are engaging in? That's a level of task absorption that can only happen when the brain blocks out other stimuli. Which is totally fine. Pinky swear. It only becomes diagnostically important when it is causing problems in our lives across life domains.[3]

Dissociation as a clinical problem that requires diagnostic attention is when our mental functioning results in the following:

- dissociative amnesia (inability to remember your own experiences and history)

- depersonalization/derealization (feeling disconnected from one's own body, thoughts, feelings, and experiences)

- identity confusion (feeling confused about who you are in the present)

- fundamental alterations of identity (feeling confused about who you are in general)

---

3 When teaching diagnostics, I always caution clinicians to look into more than one area of someone's life before offering a diagnosis. For example, please don't say a kid has oppositional defiant disorder because of how they pop off in math class when they don't pop off anywhere else. What's up in that class? Is the teacher an ass? Are they being bullied? More information required.

Have you ever come out of a movie theater having been so engrossed in something that the outside world seems weird and bright for a second? Clinically relevant levels of dissociation are like an extreme version of that that lasts more than a second. Everything seems surreal, or vague, or foggy, or as if it's happening underwater or at a great distance. The understanding of what is happening to us in the present moment doesn't register. All of these symptoms may exist within different levels of severity. And there is no pill you can take for any of this. Something happened that fundamentally changed how the world is perceived and responded to . . . by changing how the brain functions.

Basically, trauma is an acquired form of neurodiversity. Or, even more bluntly stated, a traumatic brain injury.

While the *Diagnostic and Statistical Manual* that we use to diagnose PTSD does sometimes limit who can be diagnosed and for what reasons, I think acknowledging a wider range of traumatic situations that can lead to a trauma response is important to this discussion. If you are new to the idea of viewing our responses through a trauma-informed lens, I've included an appendix on the back of the book with a general list of events that may create a trauma response. (So if you are in no way new to my books, and you already know that list quite well? You can nod your head and keep reading.)

Now, we all experience traumatic events, and not nearly all traumatic events cause traumatic stress or PTSD.

Why's that?

Basically, if we are able to make some level of sense of what happened, if we have time to heal, if we have time to grieve, if we understand that we are not to blame, we slowly get better.

But so often, none of that care is available. Or, worse, we are told we are wrong about both our experiences and our responses to them.

Because it isn't just about what happens to us, it's about how we make sense of it. It's about how we fit that experience within the context of our lives and the world around us. Dr. Gabor Maté refers to this experience throughout his documentary *The Wisdom of Trauma*. And Dialectical Behavior Therapy developer Dr. Marsha Linehan uses what I think is the perfect phrase to describe this phenomenon: *traumatic invalidation*.

Invalidation is the term we use to describe something as erroneous or untrue. If someone says it's raining when it's bright and sunny—and you point out the discrepancy with their statement and reality? You're invalidating their claim.

Invalidation also refers to a nullification based on the information being presented. You can invalidate someone's Booker Prize nomination because it turns out they plagiarized parts of their book, for example.

So what takes invalidation to the next level, making it a traumatic experience? Traumatic invalidation is what happens when we are disbelieved, discounted, or dismissed around an issue that is significant or important to us.

It can happen when a child tells their teacher that they are being abused at home and are accused of lying.

Or when a child tells their parent that they are being bullied at school and they are told to stop being dramatic and toughen up.

It could be the person who explains that they are physically ill or struggling with their emotional health and then they are told they are exaggerating, looking for attention, or making things up to get out of work.

Or someone coming out as queer or not cisgender and being told they are going through a phase, complete with deadnaming and refusal to respect pronouns.

Or someone showing they've been diagnosed with a form of neurodiversity and the response is an eyeroll and a comment that they are making an excuse for laziness.

Or when a person of color reports that someone else in their office or classroom is making racist comments and they are told they are misinterpreting what is obviously a joke.

Traumatic invalidation is not being seen, heard, believed, and understood. It may come in the form of "No, that didn't happen," or "It wasn't that bad," or even "Ok, it happened, but you are taking this all way too seriously and you need to get over it." This invalidation comes from the people who are supposed to love us and protect us. Or at least are authority figures in our lives.

Traumatic invalidation disrupts our ability to heal because it tells us *we* are invalid. That how we perceive the world and ourselves isn't correct. It violates our expectations of love, friendship, community, and care. It informs us we are excluded from experiencing support. It tells us that we are wrong to feel what we feel.

After traumatic invalidation, not only do we cease to trust the world, we also cease to trust ourselves. We experience confusion, anger, defensiveness . . . and shame. We self-abandon important aspects of who we are. We either become desperate for connection and care, even from dangerous places, or we isolate and disconnect. We seek ways of medicating the overwhelm of not being seen or not being worthy of care. So many addictions and out-of-control behaviors start as ways of coping with our perceived not-enough-ness. Because, if humans are wired for connection and those connections are weakened or severed, it impacts our lives in enormous, far-reaching ways.

And what does this have to do with dissociation? It's a result of vagal tone activation. It's a physiological means of protection when we recognize we are unsafe and unsupported. So let's review what vagal tone is a bit, yeah?

Our threat detection system allows us three physiological responses: fight, flight, or freeze.[4] This is our body recognizing the threat and choosing its best course

---

4 Please don't @ me about *fawn* being a part of this model. Fawning is a trauma response absolutely. But it's not a vagal response; it's a behavioral adaptation.

of action for escape. Not even fighting back to win, just to survive.

Do we fight our way out or haul ass on out of there?

And the freeze response? This is our body determining (generally based on past experiences) that this isn't a winnable battle and shutting down to avoid the pain we expect to be inflicted.

And THIS is dissociation. Your body is thinking it is dying. Your spirit is guarding itself while your physical self takes the hits.

This is why chronic dissociative responses are part of all trauma-related conditions. Dissociation, we now understand, is most often traumagenic (meaning trauma-induced)—with dissociative disorders having the highest rates of childhood abuse and neglect. If we were raised in (and live in) reasonably safe environments, we are able to more adequately recognize true threats from uncomfortable situations and are able to self-regulate. If you didn't have that experience, your orientation will always be self-protection, in the face of both real and perceived threats.

The more severe presentation of dissociation occurs in a diagnosis referred to as Dissociative Identity Disorder

(DID). In DID, memories are removed from their context and processed in a way that allows one to maintain a level of day-to-day functioning. This experience leads one to create alternate personas, each that have their own sense of self and independent agency. This presentation is also a potential feature of borderline personality disorder, post traumatic stress disorder, schizophrenia, schizoaffective disorder, eating disorders, panic disorders, affective disorders, obsessive-compulsive disorders, and even acute or chronic stress.

In short, the presence of dissociation is the presence of severity. It means things are so bad they can't be faced head-on anymore. It means someone is struggling greatly in ways we are not yet adept at treating effectively. And because dissociation is a frightening thing to experience (we lose confidence in our ability to engage with reality, be in control, and maintain a sense of self), it causes understandable distress that adds to the treatment struggle.

So what is going on with dissociation, and what does it have to do with shame?

One of the individuals doing cutting edge research around dissociation, trauma, and depression is psychiatrist Dr. Vedat Şar. He began terming certain forms of depression as treatment-resistant, meaning our best, Western, evidence-based practices are providing little if any symptom relief. Şar argued that these treatment-resistant forms of depression at best become something we sometimes term "double depression." Meaning chronic lower-level depression[5] with repetitive depressive episodes.

Vedat Şar noticed that this form of depression is incredibly common among people who have struggled with chronic dissociation. He observed that stressors— both internal and external—often cycle with their depressive spikes, and individuals with this presentation of depression have unique cognitive symptoms of worthlessness, guilt, and shame. And he called this experience *dissociative depression.*

And he isn't the only one who noticed this phenomenon. While Complex PTSD (C-PTSD) is not in the current edition of the *Diagnostic and Statistical Manual* (DSM-V-TR as of this writing), it does exist in the current *International Classification of Diseases* (the ICD-11 as of this writing). The difference between PTSD and

---

5 Historically, this was termed dysthymia, and, most recently, it has been termed persistent depressive disorder . . . like those of us with it didn't already know how persistent it is???

C-PTSD in the ICD (omg the acronyms, I'm so sorry) are the affective changes (changes influenced by emotions), referred to as *disturbances of self-organization*.

Which makes C-PTSD sound exactly like Dr. Şar's explanation of dissociative depression: a mood disorder that is foundationally related to (and likely caused by) a loss of self. Therefore, it doesn't respond to medications and other Western models of treatment.

Dissociation as Loss of Self

So when we talk about loss of self, we don't mean just in moments of dissociation, but continuously over days, weeks, months, years, and decades. People with C-PTSD (or dissociative depression to use Şar's term) also experience the following:

- problems in affect regulation, such as marked irritability or anger, feeling emotionally numb

- beliefs about oneself as diminished, defeated, or worthless, accompanied by feelings of shame, guilt, or failure related to the traumatic event

- difficulties in sustaining relationships and in feeling close to others

And while so many researchers and practitioners are seeing this same constellation of pain, other than "it's the trauma," we as humans often don't have a solid understanding of what is actually happening to the psyche. But Şar has us covered on that front as well, with a model proposed by himself and his colleague Erdink Ozturk.

So their theory is that we have a psychological self, the formation of who we are as an individual. And we also have our sociological self, which is the aspects of who we are that we have determined are fit for the world. Different cultures may have different acceptable sociological selves, but the idea of humans having one remains universal. Abuse, neglect, and other forms of trauma that occur during important developmental periods arrest the development of our psychological self. In other words, parts of us get locked away, hidden, and our growth is frozen—while the sociological self grows and eventually takes over completely, leading us to determine all our choices based on what is acceptable about us to the world around us.

To give you a better sense of the differences between the psychological and social selves, below are some of their contrasting properties:

Sociological Self	Psychological Self
Imitation, Modeling, Copying	Creativity
Dogmatism	Acceptance of possibilities
Vulnerability	Resilience
Conservation	Building new associations
Periods of time	Time as continuity
Shared use	Ownership
Metaphors, symbols	Signs
Single-focus awareness	Multi-focus awareness
Fixation	Progression
Adjustment	Seeking for novelty
Negotiation	Choice
Ruling and being ruled	Voluntary participation
Collectivism	Individualism
Self-seeking	Compassion
Polarization	Synthesis
Reversibility	Constancy
Aggression	Fight for survival
Eclecticism	Authenticity
Distortion	Taking a fact as it is

Table showing the properties of the sociological self vs. the psychological self.

And to be clear, a sociological self isn't a bad thing. It is how we navigate the social world after all. But in order to be emotionally healthy, our psychological self needs equal voice, otherwise reality becomes distorted. So if the psychological self has been critically wounded, the sociological self takes over to protect the wounds acquired and avoid further damage, leaving our selves out of balance.

This is all fancy talk for saying that we develop mechanisms that can manage fucked up situations—to protect us and keep us going when things are truly awful. Like many other brain-body adaptations, this protection of our psychological selves is a feature not a bug. It keeps us functioning in a relatively coherent manner and maintains a level balance between our external behavior and internal thoughts, feelings, and sensations.

But this protection of our psychological selves leads to a highly distorted worldview that remembers traumatic incidents only from the place of distortion. And this continuous fragmentation and distortion of the world leads to a dissociative self.

And here's the historically interesting part about of all this: dissociation is one of the oldest reported psychiatric disorders. Case response of dissociative disorders began appearing in the late 1700s, and by the 1800s, there were plenty of extensive descriptions of the experience.

Unfortunately, this is where we get into the dismissiveness of women's "hysteria" by physicians.

Related to this denial of the experiences of women experiencing dissociation, did you know that Freud was well aware of the extensive abuse that happened to young people in their family homes, across socioeconomic status lines? He called out his colleagues for not attending to the fact that so many young people were being molested by their fathers and other men who had access to them. In the process, he got in so much trouble for disrupting the system that paid them all, and he had to back off the topic and developed his bullshit oedipal and electra complexes instead.[6]

Because there was no traction for naming dissociation and other dysregulation what it was—a result of trauma—these experiences became dismissed by the medical establishment for decades as the behavior of people (especially women) who were "fantasy-prone" and "suggestible."

We now know dissociation is a common physiological response to trauma that 2 to 10% of people will struggle with at some point in their lives. And we now even know what process in the brain causes this phenomenon. When

6 Christina Robb's *This Changes Everything* is a fantastic read, btw.

studying chronic seizures at the Stanford Comprehensive Epilepsy Program, researchers found that patients reported an experience of dissociation before each seizure. The brain knew something bad was coming and distanced itself from the experience.

So the researchers started recording the electrical signals in the brains of the patients. They observed that the experience of dissociation started with a jump in electrical activity in the posteromedial cortex. This activity was characterized by an oscillating signal generated by nerve cells firing in coordination at 3 hertz (3 cycles per second). So weirdos that researchers are . . . they stimulated that area of the brain in the same seizure patients. And unsurprisingly, the patients would have a dissociative experience without having a seizure.

Our bestie, Dr. Şar, has also studied changes to the brain during dissociative episodes. Dr. Şar's team found that regional cerebral blood flow (rCBF) was greatly decreased in people with DID when compared with their non-DID counterparts, while more blood flow was found bilaterally in the median and superior frontal regions and occipital regions.

And a win for Team Science! Because this means, contrary to historical dismissiveness, dissociation is in fact an observable, measurable, real, and brain-based phenomenon that can and does show up in people with traumatic shame.

But if dissociation is a real and common response to our shame experiences, how do we know when it's happening?

How to Notice When We Are Dissociating Due to Our Own Shame Experiences

Dr. Jason Luoma and Dr. Jenna LeJeune founded a resource website for therapists that use principles of Acceptance and Commitment Therapy with self-compassion work, particularly in working with shame . . . as an arising emotional response, not a state of being (which is what we're up to, as well, right?).[7]

One of the approaches they suggest is to use somatic (body-based) noticing of our shame experiences.

If we are focused on our sociological selves, we are living in the reflection of a fun-house mirror . . . and often

---

7 Bonus fun fact is that Dr. Luoma published the first randomized trial of using an ACT approach to treating shame (published in the Journal of Consulting and Clinical Psychology in 2011).

start responding to our shame experiences without even realizing that is what we are doing.

But our bodies still know what's happening, and somatic noticing is a process we can use to see when shame is activated within us.

So when you start paying attention to your body in relational situations, you are looking for the somatic experiences that tell you that you are reacting as if *you* are a contagion. Common bodily sensations may include:

- shaking

- trembling

- flushing

- elevated heartbeat

- elevated breathing patterns

- nausea

- sinking stomach

- tight chest

- muscular tension

- any sensations that are related to things no longer feeling real, which includes derealization (a feeling that one's surroundings are not real), depersonalization (a feeling that oneself is not real), and dissociation (a disconnection from all aspects of one's immediate experience)

Once we start noticing the somatic patterns, we can better capture the thoughts and feelings that run alongside them.

In other words, what is the emotional fallout that your brain uses to interpret your bodily sensations? This could include anxiety, fear, anger, embarrassment, self-recrimination, guilt, sadness, a sense of isolation, or a sense of rejection.

Once we answer this question—once we know the emotion that follows the body-based response—we can then trace the self-talk interpretations of those feelings. We can ask, "What am I thinking when I am feeling the above feelings?" This could include recriminations directed at self or others, such as "I'm such a dumbass!" or "They're such a bitch!"

Ok, great. And now—because yes, we are working backwards on purpose . . . processing bottoms-up instead of top-down—what was the situation that instigated the experience that led to the feelings in your body, that led to the above self-talk?

And what were your response impulses to the instigating situation (yes, all of the responses your brain suggested, whether you acted a fool or not)? In other words, what were you inclined to do? Did you follow through or choose a different behavior?

And then finally, what was the outcome of your behavioral choices? (And yes, doing nothing is a choice ...so what happened when you did nothing, if that's what you did?)

Ok, now that we have a process—with questions—to notice our dissociation due to shame, we can turn our attention to where we've been so far and look forward to how we can go about healing that shame.

WHERE DOES ALL THIS LEAVE US?

Hey there. How ya doin'?

That was a lot, and we haven't even gotten to the *getting better* part yet.

In order to unfuck our own mental health issues, the "why" is vital. Which meant spending the first part of this book looking at the lesser-known research on shame as an emotional state and not a personality-bound trait. And then, looking at all the research on unhealed trauma leading to more shame experiences that are treated (erroneously, despite good intentions) as depressive disorders.

And all that??? *waves hands in the air like the over-enthusiastic college professor that I am* is important and needful information. Because it explains the loss of balance between our true self (the psychological self) and what we show the world for safety (the sociological self), as the emotion of shame is continuously reinforced and validated as something we deserve to experience.

I mean, it's not true.

We don't deserve shame. And we can even know that intellectually.

But in this particular whirlpool of events and memories and continuous reinforcement? If your acceptance in the world relies on how you are viewed and your perceptions of how you are viewed, you can never heal. Only the psychological self, an intact human psyche, can heal from depression.

And, as mentioned in the above pages, our treatment approaches almost always fail because the distortions and resulting dissociation aren't accounted for.

Because of this, the second half of this book is going to be even less Western in healing approaches than usual.

Because ancestral healers were attending to shame-in-context. They were doing work to help their community heal. And much of it was incredibly powerful processes.

Also, working with shame isn't entirely out of the spectrum of Western psychology. Back in the 1960s,

Donald Winnicott, a psychoanalyst and pediatrician, was speaking to the importance of authenticity (an intact psychological self) in humans, recognizing that shame strips our ability to be authentic. He argued that shame becomes a hidden injury, protected by a false self.

And as we talked about earlier, Donald Nathanson developed his compass of shame model in 1992, as a means of describing the common shame responses in humans. He laid out four ways we typically work with shame: withdrawal, avoidance, attack self, and/or attack others. More recently, we can see the influence of his shame compass in Brené Brown's methods for building shame resilience, which include recognizing shame and what triggers it within us, building awareness of the influences that induce shame, naming it when it occurs, and reaching out to others when that happens.

And all this begs the question: "Ok, but how?"

The good news is we aren't near the first people asking this question. There's a path here that involves looking at ancestral treatment methodologies and bringing them back into practice. This is where shadow work and soul retrieval come into play.

So let's get (just the tiniest bit) weird.

Part 2:
Healing
Shame

*I*f shame is a function of trauma—imprinted and reinforced by dissociation from our psychological self, creating a sense of self as contagion—how the fuck do you even work with something that damn heavy?

Well, for that job, we're gonna use some old, tried-and-true tools. Like really old. We're gonna explore frankly ancient healing practices. Over the centuries, society has changed—but humans haven't really—so we are going to work with principles that, in modern parlance, have been termed *shadow work* and *soul retrieval*.

THE SCIENCE AND ART OF SHADOW WORK

S hadow work is basically the process of making conscious the aspects of ourselves that we have hidden from view. The stuff we can call the "unconscious" or the "preconscious" or whatever. The stuff we know, but we don't "know."

Specifically, when I reference the shadow in shadow work, I'm using these terms the way psychiatrist Carl Jung did. He chose *shadow* to describe the aspects of ourselves that we hid because they were considered unpalatable to those around us.

But those parts we hide aren't just our darker impulses, like me wanting to haul off and punch the guy who was texting while driving in the rain this morning. The shadow is also our quirkiness, our oddities, our excitement, our joy, our infodumping nerdom, our chatter, and any other thing that those around us found bothersome and asked us to tuck away.

I say *hide* on purpose, because we only *think* we are discarding supposedly intolerable things about ourselves. (In other words, over-identifying with our sociological self over our psychological self.) But those hidden parts don't really go away. Anything that makes us who we are remains a part of us in some way, shape, or form. Hence, the term *shadow*—always with us, but not always visible.

This hiding of our shadow starts as conscious and becomes less and less so over time. Eventually, the shadow becomes all the parts we have become unaware of within ourselves. This happens because we have moved these aspects of who we are into a space that we rarely access with conscious awareness.

This process happens because these hidden things are our most fragile parts. And to protect every part of ourselves, we present only the approved parts of our personality, in hopes of avoiding further pain, injury, and rejection. This might even look like developing a completely alternative personality in order to be accepted by those around us.

Either way, eventually, the adaptations we make consciously become preconscious. Decisions we made as responses turn into beliefs about who we are in the world. Simply put, we internalize the voices of not-enoughness.

But it gets even bigger than the individual level. The shadow also has an epigenetic component.

That lineage of pain and unbelonging that was never healed in our ancestors? That's something else we carry forward. This is why our own healing is so important. We are healing not only for ourselves, but for those around us, those who come after us . . . and those who came before.

So, to begin this healing process, let's start with a deeper understanding of the human shadow and why it is such an important part of healing shame.

How Shadow Work Connects Us to Our Authentic Self

Carl Jung may have died in 1961, but his work continues to be directly influential on our understanding of the human psyche. Of particular note here is his influence on transpersonal psychology—which is just a fancy term for all of the states of consciousness that exist beyond the personal level of our psyche.

In other words, transpersonal psychology refers to what exists in three areas:

1. our *personal unconscious* (the information which informs how we interact with ourselves and the world)

2. the *collective unconscious* (all of our ancestral wisdom and knowledge that is shared by all humanity across time)

3. how we interact with *cultural archetypes* (the themes and patterns that exist within people throughout history)

We're mostly focusing on our personal unconscious as we do shame repair work, but you will notice the themes of both connection to others and broad human patterns of behavior within this work as well, as they all interplay within our lifespan.

So, as we already reviewed, the personal unconscious is comprised significantly of the shadow, which is the part of our psyche that we consider negative and undesirable, but this part still functions as part of a greater whole. Wanna nerd out? Simple version looks like this:

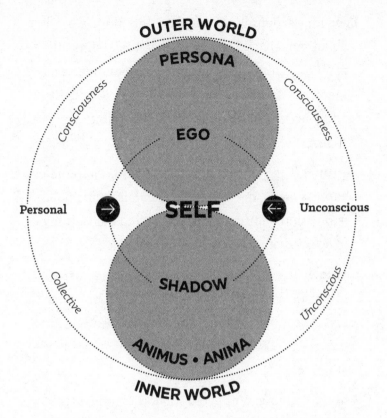

Visual depiction of how Jung breaks down the inner and outer world

Feel like you're too complicated? Complication was Jung's jam and life's work; you aren't the only complicated human. We can handle this, even with his weird linguistic choices, no worries.

Let's look at the basics of what this all means. According to Jung:

Ego: Jung's definition refers to the story we tell about ourselves. The ego is how Jung defines the conscious mind: all of our thoughts, emotions, and memories that we are aware of. It's our identity and our understanding of our storyline across time.

Persona: The persona is our outward, simplified expression of the ego. It's essentially our public expression of our personality . . . and our training to be obedient to expectations (ugh).

Shadow: The shadow is a purely emotional aspect of our personality—that lies in opposition to the ego. According to Jung, the shadow lies outside the conscious mind and has its own level of autonomy.

Anima-Animus: Within our shadow, Jung identified that there are qualities we might culturally and traditionally think of as belonging only to individuals of the gender opposite of our own. Jung described the traditionally-understood-to-be-female aspects as the anima and the traditionally-understood-to-be-male aspects the animus. He felt it important to integrate both aspects of our personality, in order for us to be fully whole and authentic. (Jung didn't write about individuals who existed outside of the gender binary. I would say that anyone who exists in a more gender fluid state has brought forth a deep and conscious awareness of their anima and animus and lived this truth within their everyday expression of ego through persona.)

Self: Jung referred to a person who has overcome the limitations of their persona, recognized their ego-consciousness, and moved beyond it to embrace their shadow (as well as their anima/animus balance) to be a person who has the capacity to reach their full potential (Jung referred to it as "the God within us"). That's a lot of words and complicated concepts. Basically, just think of the self as being you at your most authentic, before life imposed so many weird rules and conformity notions on you that you couldn't even remember who you were born to be.

All these ideas aside . . . Jung himself often stated that people were overthinking the term *shadow*. He would remind people that the shadow is all that is preconscious in our minds. Jung said, "Until you make the unconscious

conscious, it will direct your life and you will call it fate."
In other words, and related to our shame healing journey:
when we repress pain—repress our emotional self that
balances our public-facing self—we cause continued
harm to ourselves and others.

But when we do the opposite—when we engage with
our shadow through shadow work:

1. We are less likely to engage in destructive
   behaviors.

2. We have better boundaries with those around us.

3. Our relationships are better because we better
   understand and accept ourselves and others.

4. Our communication skills improve.

5. Our physical health improves because we are not
   carrying the types of psychic pain that creates
   inflammatory damage in the body.

Shadow Work Meditation

I know, I know. Here I am already asking you to try stuff.
Of course you don't have to do a damn thing you don't
wanna do, cuz why would you take orders from a book?
But if you are amenable . . . I am hoping you'll find this
meditation useful as a means of first contact with your

shadow. It's gentle, honoring, and not asking anything from the exchange, except an offering of peaceful recognition.

Specifically, this type of meditation is referred to as a "metta meditation." *Metta* loosely translates to loving-kindness. In essence, it's a focus of general goodwill, friendliness, and open-heartedness. It's a way of engaging in the world without all shields up, feeling defensive and ill at ease.

A metta meditation involves focusing not just on the breath, but on a series of healing statements about yourself, another person or group of people, or the world.

The original texts from the Buddha on metta (as translated from *The Discourse on Loving-Kindness*) is . . .

Wishing: In gladness and in safety, may all beings be at ease.

Whatever living beings there may be, omitting none

Let none deceive another, or despise any being in any state

Let none through anger or ill will wish harm upon another.

These statements may have an archaic language (and don't worry, we're gonna use a more modern format), but they speak to universal human struggles across time. Specifically, the harm we experience just by being a human living in an imperfect world, and the continued harm (suffering) that we impose on ourselves in the process. Metta meditation allows us to work with the feelings we avoid the most, like aversion and despair. The Buddha stated that by working with uncomfortable emotions, we can transform them into something that serves us better.

And we should also offer metta to ourselves. Self-hatred is far more common than hatred of others. Buddhist meditation instructor Sharon Salzberg discusses how this is super common in Western culture as an offset of systemic oppression (defined by bell hooks as "imperialist white supremacist capitalist patriarchy"). Because no matter what set of circumstances or privileges we have accessed, no one measures up to our oppressive system's standards. We all struggle with not-enough-ness and feel a continuous need to earn our space in the world, rather than recognizing that we deserve care by the sheer fact that we are human.

The purpose of this meditation is a deeper connection to our inner world instead of the outer one, by reaching out to the disowned parts of ourselves. The unconscious parts. The shadow parts. It's a first step in inviting these parts back into the full self—telling them they are also loved, valued, and wanted.

Focusing on the shadow with which we are looking to connect, here are some more modernized metta meditation statements that you can use in your own practice. You can say these out loud or think them in your head, timed with your breath.

- May my shadow be protected and safe from harm from others

- May my shadow be protected and safe from self-inflicted harm

- May my shadow be happy

- May my shadow body support the practice of loving awareness

- May my shadow be free from anxiety

- May my shadow be free from anger

- May my shadow be free from fear

- May my shadow love itself exactly as it is

- May my shadow be free from suffering

- May my shadow find peace within me

- May my shadow find peace in the larger world

- May my shadow find balance between attachment and apathy

You may find that expressing warmth and openness and positive regard to the shadow, was more difficult than you thought. Connecting to what had to be hidden and denied can feel dysregulating. Or even straight-up wrong. Like you are going against very early childhood instructions.

But even the impulses of our shadow selves that we don't want running the show? You know the parts that are protective but unskillful, if we are using clinical language . . . or petty and ratchet if we aren't? They exist for a reason. And it gets harder and harder to be un-petty and un-ratchet if you don't honor what these impulses serve. So let's look at that.

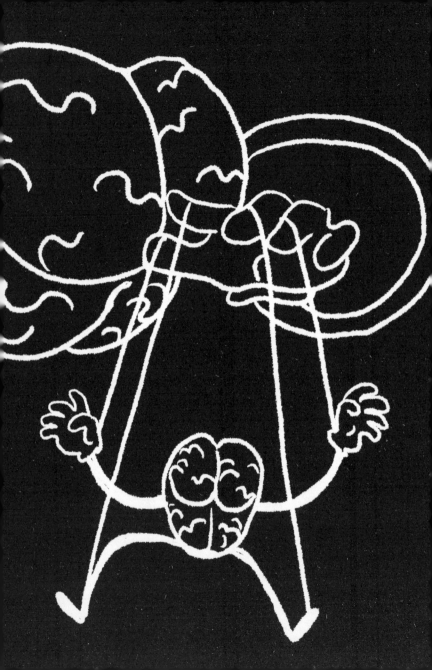

WHAT IS THE POINT OF THE SHADOW?

*T*o protect you. Full stop, really. The point of the shadow is your safety and security. If we are going to tie it into vagal tone stuff, the shadow holds the parts of us that activate our sympathetic nervous system response. You know, all the fight-flight-freeze ish that means we are expecting some sort of fight.

One of the best metaphors of shadow work I've read is to consider the shadow a baby rattlesnake. Rattlesnakes have the ability to hunt and kill at a week old, even before they have their warning rattle. But they are still small and vulnerable and more likely to perceive a situation as one where they need to fight back. And while they don't have as much venom in their bodies to use with prey yet, some evidence suggests the venom they do have is more toxic.[8]

8 I'm not a herpetologist nor do I play one on TV. It's a metaphor. Please, no need to @ me about this either, thx.

The baby rattlesnake, then, like the shadow, isn't skillful in reactions or providing the body what it needs to manage a situation. Because the shadow doesn't have experience managing a difficult situation proactively, it overreacts and overloads our system with all kinds of stress hormones and the like.

If you've ever felt like you were just in a total chaos, irrational mindset?

If you were just feral in your response? Defensive and unskillful? Petty and ratchet?

That might have been the shadow. It will wear itself out trying to manage the fear of exposure (and resulting pain) that it expects.

Simply put, the shadow wants power and control, but can't achieve either through mature means. Because it has been hidden for so long, it doesn't know how to act responsibly when it emerges from the depths, which can result in some pretty fucked up and increasingly long-term consequences, which we'll get into now.

Consequences of Our Fragmentation

The great irony in all this, is that the more we try to control the shadow, the more it ends up controlling us. Because who we are is still in there, imprisoned and shame-filled, young like a baby rattlesnake . . . and worried about being misunderstood and being punished. And those early and traumatic memories tend to be the emotional space we operate from—instead of our executive-function-thinking-brain that keeps us smiling and nodding at our boss so we don't lose our jobs for having a melt down. But our little-kid-wounded-self is melting down in the background as we-in-the-present feel increasingly unsafe and unraveled.

This feeling of unsafety leads us to respond by doubling down on keeping the shadow under lock and key. Which continues to shower hurt and pain in our lives, because we are fundamentally out of balance. It's like our own body becomes a holding cell of increasingly angry, hostile, and frantic individuals clamoring for attention and relief and care. We have to carry that within ourselves while continuing to smile and nod at whatever we are supposed to be smiling and nodding at. And the more we carry in the shadow, the less energy we have to live life.

And because the shadow is so loud and unwieldy in its attempts to get our attention, it remains the strongest force in our lives. The things we have learned to **not** want for ourselves become the biggest part of us—which will continue to be true if we don't engage with the shadow in the dungeon, whose strategies are to protect us, capture our attention, and remind us: *We can't heal what we pretend doesn't exist.*

In other words, yes, we must work with the shadow.

WHAT DO YOU MEAN BY "DOING SHADOW WORK"? PRACTICALLY?

So how does one "do" shadow work? It's self-reflection work, which means journaling, meditation, and other means of processing. Ugh, I know, I'm so sorry. Haven't figured out a way around it. And here's why: Shadow work is the process of reconnecting to (and taking accountability for) the parts of ourselves that we have been trained to deny.

At first, when we do this denial/hiding process, we are aware of it. As in: *Don't be loud or silly or goofy . . . the adults find it irritating and call you a bad kid.* But eventually those external voices become our own internal dialogue. And we continue to suppress anything about ourselves that we perceive as loud/silly/goofy/generally unwanted. Again, the shadow is made up of the parts of our personality we had to discard.

But paying attention to what we have learned to ignore (for years, if not decades) can feel very overwhelming. Every alarm bell in your body is going to struggle against the process. Your nervous system may scream "Danger Will Robinson," while flailing about. Or may shut down completely. This is normal. And it sucks. And the only way I have found through the process . . . is to just keep slogging through the process. It's finding all the pieces that have been discarded and bringing them back into the whole. Yes, even the dark parts.

It doesn't mean letting yourself connect to every selfish instinct and being a big ol' asshole. Whether it is truly dark or just perceived as dark, it is important to attend to everything that has influence in your life. Of learning to live alongside your own emotional pain. Simply put, shadow work is about honoring everything about who you are and living a full and wholly integrated life.

What makes this so incredibly difficult to do is that it requires radical self-honesty. In a society that has worked hard to train you out of such reflexivity.

So let's take a moment to practice the self-compassion that is what allows us to engage fully with self-honesty.

Compassionate Letter to the Shadow

Just like the loving-kindness meditation this exercise is also designed to soften our stance to our shadows in a conscious way. Writing a compassionate letter to yourself is a key activity of self-compassion work. In this process, all we are doing is shifting the focus to the shadow part of ourselves.

But this isn't a huge commitment of a project. Even if you only do this activity once, it's still hella valuable (and again, no side-eye if you don't do it at all . . . this book is for your process, so skip anything that doesn't relate). But ideally, the UC Berkeley's Greater Good Science Center suggests doing this kind of exercise as a daily practice for at least a week, then moving on to make it a weekly or monthly practice. Kinda think of it as a strategic form of self-care, like going to the dentist and moving your body more.

An important note: This isn't an hours-long process; it shouldn't take you more than ten to fifteen minutes. No one is going to see it unless you want them to, so don't worry about it being sloppy or grammatically challenged or anything else that may slow you down.

With all that groundwork laid, here are the basic steps to writing a compassionate letter to your shadow:

1. Reflect on the fact that there are aspects of yourself you found necessary to hide away in order to be accepted. You don't have to be specific when you first start out, but as you do shadow work, you may find particular aspects you want to focus on . . . like having a loud, joyful laugh that you were told was irritating or something like that—basically, anything about who you are that you have been told (explicitly or implicitly) is wrong with you.

2. Now, reflect on how this "wrongness" made you feel about yourself. Sad? Angry? Ashamed?

3. Now, write a letter to that shadow part expressing compassion and empathy for how difficult it is to exist in this space of being unwanted. Even if you are focusing on an aspect of yourself that isn't of benefit to you behaviorally (like yelling at people when you are upset, for example . . . not a skillful way of expressing our pain generally), show compassion, understanding, and acceptance. Not to let unskillful behaviors continue, but to recognize where they come from so they can be honored and released as you learn more and do

things differently. Be honest with yourself, but good to yourself.

Because this is one of those simple-but-not-easy tasks, you can use some of the below tips to get you started if you feel stuck.

1. Write from the viewpoint of someone who loves and accepts you. The kind bestie who loves you enough to say, "I totally get it." They may also say, "Let's do better," but they don't attack your personhood in the process.

2. Remind yourself we have no remedy for imperfection. Everyone has things about themselves that they are unhappy with or they have hidden away from themselves and those around them. And chances are, there are many other people struggling with something quite similar.

3. Consider how events in your life (yes, traumatic ones, but even just generally cruddy ones) may impact these struggles. Not as an excuse, but as an assistance to explanation. As in, "It makes sense that *this* would be my response. My family always

avoided discussing uncomfortable feelings, so it's so much harder for me now."

4. Then, ask yourself what could help you cope better or be more skillful when these aspects of yourself show up. Not as a judgment of "ugh, I suck," but in a frame of "I want to be happier, healthier, and more connected, and this might help my healing."

Shame hides in the shadows (see what I did there?) and self-compassion brings everything back into the light. If we learn to dial down the self-criticism, what has been relegated to the shadow can begin to re-emerge for integration.

This is one of those activities that seems a little silly on the surface (or maybe a lot silly, depending on who you are), but is incredibly powerful and healing if you give it a real try. It shows up in my books on the regular, because it's something I have found to be consistently helpful for the people with whom I work . . . and in my own shadow work.

WHY SHADOW WORK MATTERS

*A*s we continue our journey into shadow work, it's important to keep our why front and center. Because this shit is hard. It is. But everything you have been going through is even tougher. And you deserve the chance to face these issues and begin your healing.

As we know, it doesn't work to hold your shadow hostage or deny it. Since childhood, your ability to hide your shadow is what your shadow has been counting on, so it can continue working to keep you feeling invulnerable and safe. In adulthood, however, the cost of hiding becomes too high: losing intimacy, closeness, trust, and security with others. But when we can call our shadow by name when it rises up, we can take productive and healing action.

Because healing isn't a mechanism of self-punishment. The banishment of the shadow—an integral part of yourself—is punishment. Integration back into the whole is healing. In integration, you build ways of having more accountability in your life while lessening your suffering. You have access to so much previously lost energy to do this work.

And that healing and learning process invites us to become fully authentic human beings. We learn what we no longer need to tolerate. And we also learn tolerance that was missing in other situations because we were so busy managing the shame that would emerge when our shadow was threatened.

So how do we find that frightened shadow and coax it out into the light?

Recognizing the Shadow

It can be difficult to recognize when our shadow aspects are banging against the bars of their prison. Pain doesn't always show up like sadness or retreat. It can look like irritation, anger, or rage. It can look like anxiety, depression, and other forms of illness. It can look like a hyper need for control, perfectionism, withdrawal from others, or entire dependence on others. Figuring out how your shadow presents is the first step.

This means paying attention to yourself metacognitively. Meaning noticing what the brain is doing. Consider: How do you present when faced with something challenging, like loss, disappointment, or conflict? Do you get quiet and sad? Defensive and argumentative? Confused and shut down?

Our stress-defaults are our best window into the nature of our own particular shadows. The shadow isn't something inherent (something we are born with), right? It's a protective *something* that emerges based on our overarching culture, family dynamics, intrapersonal experiences, and so on.

Because of our individuality, we each experience different things as being "wrong" with us and we all create our own systems for suppressing these impulses in order to avoid displeasing others. Eventually, these systems crystalize within us and begin to feel more like "us" than our actual selves.

But making real and sustained changes in our lives means honoring every aspect of who we are. As much as we'd like to avoid it, the energy of the shadow is necessary for repair.

But this can be a scary thought. In fact, one of the biggest fears most people have about doing shadow work is that they will unleash some primitive, destructive, monstrous force within them. Because, of course! We have been told over and over that those hidden parts are bad impulses that can only cause pain.

But these impulses aren't inherently evil, or out of our control, because they are being acknowledged. The shadow can be destructive, but only when ignored.

Because every part of our personality we don't love will act out with hostility to us. And we can only heal with awareness. Once we know how and why we struggle, we can begin to make different choices.

The anthropologists whose work in this field I have most aligned with are Ashley Montagu and Riane Eisler. Both wrestled with the complexity of being human in ways I respect. Dr. Montagu noted that yes-of-course-absolutely humans have aggressive instincts. They are part of or genetic inheritance. But aggressive instincts aren't a demand for violent behavior. Violence is often learned, and often in our families of origin.

Dr. Eisler explained our humanist capacities using two groups of our relatives, chimpanzees and bonobos. I won't unpack all of her research around the topic (but if you are a fellow big ol' nerd, definitely read her books), but the idea is we have the socially aggressive, power-over chimpanzee energy and the mellow, chill, power-with (and bisexual AF, which doesn't hurt) bonobo energy— both within our DNA.

And we can curate bonobo energy as easily as we can chimpanzee energy. If we think that we must suppress our chimp energy into the shadow, we are always fighting those instincts. Instead of recognizing them, knowing they are available for our protection in a true crisis . . . but also that we and those around us are much better served by showing compassion, connection, and community care.

But, as we've discussed, punishing the chimp instincts doesn't result in peace and solid emotional health. Pinky swear. Once we take the monster costume off of our shadow, we find the parts of us that are small and sad and vulnerable. Then, we can reparent those parts of ourselves in the ways we needed to be treated originally.

(And—don't worry—we are going to look at all the ways we can work with these instincts without letting them run around stabbing everyone in their path.)

To start, we can consider the following: What are some ways your shadow self gets revealed in everyday life? Let's look at some possibilities:

Projection: You find yourself projecting personality traits and uncomfortable traits you experience onto others. (And the ghost of Freud says, "Dayuuummm, ok.")

Hair Trigger Temper: Your anger reaction time is super quick, at least in certain situations.

Injured Party: You don't see avenues of self-advocacy when others perpetuate harm against you.

Permeable Boundaries: You have a hard time saying no (and/or sticking to it) and often let people take advantage of you.

Patterns of Out-of-Control Behaviors and Addictions: Pretty self-explanatory, right? You are avoiding and medicating **something.**

Faux Stoicism: You find yourself denying certain emotions (even to yourself), rather than let yourself experience your authentic feelings.

Now that we've started this path of inquiry, let's look at possible activities that will allow you to connect to your shadow.

Spelunking For Shadow Parts: Witnessing Adaptations

Once we start internalizing the "rules of engagement" we were exposed to, it can be difficult to realize/recognize where we adapt ourselves for safety and belonging. With this exercise, you won't find every adaptation example in your shadow, especially not right off the bat. But start with the goal of paying attention to patterns of your own behavior when it feels (or has felt) inauthentic. That first step helps us start finding aspects of our own shadows.

As you are able to open the hatch and find out what all has been living in the shadow, the following questions may help enter the dark cave of the shadow. Consider these questions as a guide as you spelunk for those shadow parts/adaptations:

• Who were the people you relied upon for (or hoped for from) love, connection, and belonging? Where did you make sacrifices to please these people (or avoid displeasing them)?

- What did you have to do to "earn" acceptance?

- How have these habits carried through to today?

- Now, think about the things that feel like authentic security. What thoughts or ideas do you have about yourself that bring you back to authenticity? What about you gives you a sense of peace and freedom? What is authentic to your spirit?

If these questions aren't provoking any or many aha moments for you, you can also reflect on any the following:

- In which aspects of your life are you struggling?

- What emotions, people, or situations do you find yourself trying to avoid?

- In what way did traumatic/adverse events from your childhood impact how you live today?

- How do your insecurities show up? What do you not like about yourself? How do you think others see you?

- What dreams have you had that upset you the most? What happened within them?

- If you could erase one memory what would it be?

- What aspects of your life are most disconcerting to you?

- What kinds of issues are you most likely to hold grudges about?

- What have you held a grudge about the longest?

- Which kinds of irrational fears are most likely to hold you back? Which irrational fear has been the biggest barrier to you recently?

- What are your bad habits? What prevents you from "breaking" them?

- What kinds of lies do you tell yourself?

- In what ways are you regularly hypocritical?

- What is the biggest promise you've made to yourself that you broke?

- What relationships do you hold on to that are unhealthy?

- In what other ways do you self-sabotage?

Capturing the Shadow: An Activity Where You Are Allowed to Vent as Much as You Want

I've had a few clients work with this activity and find it incredibly eye-opening.

Unfortunately, it is one of those things you have to have a presence of mind to do in the middle of an emotional moment; fortunately, cell phones have made the equipment part of the process far easier.

Basically, all you need to do is record yourself when experiencing big emotions. Say what you really want to say in the moment. In your out-loud voice, say everything that comes to mind. No matter how ratchet and shitty and mean and sabotage-y it is. We are looking for patterns, not evidence that you are a shitty person. Thinking things in the moment doesn't mean you value these ideologies; instead, we are only looking for how the shadow acts out when it has a chance. That's all. No judgment or catastrophes here.

When you hear the recording, listen for clues about how (1) you are asking for permission or (2) aiming to please. Then, afterward, spend time reflecting on your modes of expression to better understand the parts of you that have been activated. While this can be a fucking hard process, hearing your shadow speak has the power to connect you to your early fears and needs in a moment of tension.

Finding Your Shadow through Others

To start this activity, visualize a hypercritical person. It could be someone from your past (maybe someone that you thought about when unpacking some of your shame responses from earlier in the book) or someone in your present. But it can be anyone who activates insecurity and self-consciousness within you.

(If the idea of doing so is really activating for you, use a technique from Internal Family Systems and imagine them behind a two-way mirror. You can see them, but they can't see you, unless you flip a switch to let them.)

Now, look at yourself from what you perceive is their point of view. What do you look like to them? Describe what you are visualizing concretely.

- What do you look like?

- What do you sound like?

- How do you behave?

- In what ways do you disappoint them, anger them, or sadden them?

This projection will likely align with your shadow.

Integration of the Shadow: A Meditation

This is a simple exercise designed to help you center and focus so you can attend to what your body is trying to communicate. This activity is a gentle opportunity to observe your shadow and what it is saying to you about yourself.

Start by taking some deep abdominal breaths.

Feel into your uncomfortable emotion. Where is it in your body? What sensations are you experiencing?

Ask yourself, "What are these emotions and sensations trying to teach me? What do I need to understand about this situation?"

Let your sensations and emotions move and shift. Notice what they do with curiosity instead of judgment.

Jot down any observations you made or insights you had.

How to Bond with Your Shadow

Once you have done some work identifying your shadow, the next step is to re-bond with these aspects of yourself. You can continue to use the loving-kindness meditation and the compassionate letter project to soothe and welcome it (in fact, I hope you do!), but this activity is designed to take the specific found aspects of your shadow and reconnect with them.

And don't worry if you suspect there are some aspects of yourself that are so deeply hidden none of these techniques are helping you find them. We will work with those energies in the next part of this book. We're going to get even more woo-woo before we're done!

After you've done the exercises from earlier about building a more concrete understanding of your shadow, take this conceptualization of it and communicate the following:

1. You belong with me—we are part of each other.

2. You are wanted and welcome, always.

3. You are necessary for my survival.

4. You are necessary for my growth.

5. You are necessary for my happiness.

6. You are with me at all times.

When repeating these statements to yourself, feel into your body where your shadow can rest. This will allow you to work with your shadow, even when your impulses are counterproductive. You can communicate in the future by asking:

- What are you needing me to know?

- What are you wanting from me?

- How are you hoping I will handle this situation?

WHAT IF SHADOW WORK IS ONLY THE STARTING POINT?

*F*irst of all, thank you for hanging in with me on some exercises that may have felt a little weird. My hope is that you connected to parts of yourself that have felt too unsafe to acknowledge, let alone embrace. Much of our experiences of the world, post-trauma, are that of preventing more pain. Of fitting in—of figuring out what everyone wants us to be and endeavoring to be just that.

When in reality we can only be the best possible version of ourselves. And that requires being our full selves to begin with.

Whatever insights you noticed, patterns you clocked, questions you have about the shadow work are important. Even ones that may seem less important at this point in your life. You can keep notes on any app or in any journal you own. Because recognizing these aspects of self may be all it takes to bring them back into the light.

But in other cases, the shame around them may have been so toxic that finding them all and inviting them home requires a level of work that was historically called *soul retrieval.*

THE SCIENCE AND ART OF ALTERED CONSCIOUSNESS AND SOUL RETRIEVAL

Shadow work may be "enough" for some people to grow and connect with their psychological self to achieve healing. But so many of us read about the damage caused by shame and trauma and recognize how deep those wounds are within us. Which leads us to the somewhat more complex, deeper work of soul retrieval, which is based in our ancient understanding of the need for ritual. So, real quick, let's science the shit out of what rituals mean first.

How Rituals Work

Ritual work may seem weird and woo-woo to many people. (Both researchers and normies.) We don't often think of ritual with a level of intellectual rigor. Even when rituals are studied by scientists, it's usually anthropologists working to understand a culture different from their own.

Is understanding cultures different from our own important and necessary work? Fuck, yes. But only as long as we do it in ways that aren't othering. This includes comparing and ranking modernity. Friendly reminder: different doesn't mean more primitive (but is often treated as if it does).

So many ritual practices are perceived and framed as symbolic. Benign at best. Primitive (as mentioned), silly, or even dangerous at worst. This is because, again, rituals themselves aren't approached with the intellectual rigor it takes to understand their true, culturally embedded meaning. Trust me, as someone who has seen enormous misrepresentations of her own culture in historical works[9] and whose own dissertation was designed to combat much misinfo.

And I'm not the only person to call bullshit, and not near the smartest person to do so. Anthropologist

9 "Hahahaha, those Choctaw were sun worshippers!" Well, no. Farmers. Not just hunters and gatherers. We're farmers. Which makes the sun . . . kinda important? And if you are creating weird mystical translations of another society's everyday language? You're gonna make something super pragmatic suddenly very weird and mysterious. One of my favorite examples of this was a painted stone I saw at a museum dedicated to some local cave drawings. The stone was clearly a compass but was marked as a religious artifact. Nahullo nonsense.

Don Handelman, in reviewing both his research and interpretations of events, as well as that of colleagues, formulated a theory about what rituals *really* do. Which is . . . work. In their own right.

He's not the only person to say so. For example, Deepak Chopra's *Quantum Healing* and Jerome Frank's *Persuasion & Healing*, as well as many other rigorously researched books, talk about the effectiveness of the placebo effect. We tend to disparage this effect as "thinking about things helps pretend we are better" instead of recognizing that our belief in the process activates the healing we are looking to undergo. *So it really does help.*

I especially like Dr. Handelman's framework delineated in his book *Models and Mirrors* as an explanation for the phenomenon. He uses the term *models* to explain how rituals are models of the transformation we are looking to undergo. The *mirrors* in question are our understanding of larger society and how culture is understood and expressed. We engage with these frameworks to care for ourselves and others and meet our needs for wellness.

All therapeutic practices, really, are rituals of healing. The aforementioned Jerome Frank stated that therapy works because both the clinician and client believe the process to be helpful and create a relationship designed to have healing occur. Researcher Bruce Wampold set out to prove or disprove Dr. Frank's theory by doing a meta-analytic[10] study of a bunch of different treatment approaches to find out which was the best.

And, no surprise: there isn't a best approach (no matter what the hype men of CBT and EMDR tell you). Instead, the study showed that the effectiveness of different methods was determined by the common factors of the relationship. Not the therapy tools themselves, but the context in which they are used.

Basically, if an intervention makes sense to you and you are hopeful that it will help? It quite probably will.

This is a long way of saying that the work I have found to be most helpful for individuals drowning in shame and shame-adjacent emotions? It doesn't come from modern treatment paradigms. The most helpful strategies I've found are based on our less modern ways of knowing—ways that are relationship-focused. And I believe that is exactly why they work better than other methods in this case.

---

10 Meta-analysis is where you (essentially) squish a bunch of different studies together and re-run the stats as a conglomerate study.

WORKING WITH SOUL RETRIEVAL

*T*know, I know—your first thought (and maybe second through seventh thoughts) is that I am getting even weirder than usual. I mean, maybe. But likely, this section will make enormous sense to your healing journey once I explain what I mean by soul loss and soul retrieval.

Among my people, the Choctaw, the concept of soul in the Judeo-Christian sense did not exist. In pre-colonized Chahta culture, we were known to have an inner spirit (*shilup*, which has been modernized to mean "ghost") and an outer spirit (*shilombish*, which has been modernized to mean "soul"). Shilup is our whole, intact, and complete essence of self, and the part of us that travels to the beyond upon our death. Shilombish is the essence that creates our human embodiment. It is the part that may remain behind after our death if there was unfinished business surrounding our life and/or death.

In this dual-soul model, there is always a part of us that remains whole and complete and unbroken. But there is another part of us that can be damaged by pain and tragedy in our lives—in ways that diminish our humanity. So when I reference soul loss and soul retrieval, that is what I think of: the pain that shilombish faces when harm befalls us. And this is the part we can work to heal in the present in order to be our most full and authentic selves.

If you have had experiences of religious trauma, the idea of shilombish may be a framework that is more consistent with your worldview. Spirituality, if done well, is a way of building connection, whereas religion is regularly weaponized to demand compliance.

But hey, if *soul* doesn't do it for you, you can use any other term you want for the part of you we'll be working with: your essence of self, your energetic self, or any other way you conceptualize the you-ness that is more than the sum of your parts. Anywhere I use the term *soul* or *shilombish*, feel free to scratch it out and insert your own word. (As long as you own the copy of this book in your hands, that is. Please don't have your local librarian come for me.)

Shilombish experiences traumatic events, as much as every other system of our body. When a situation is too painful to tolerate, parts of ourselves will simply leave. They get buried deep within the shadow.

Remember all that stuff about dissociation? That's the modern term for this lost aspect of self. Soul loss is just a different cultural term. Whatever you call it, it's a self-protective response to pain. Because the pain is too excruciating to be processed in the moment, part of shilombish moves away in order to keep us from having to experience the full impact of the traumatic event.

Have you ever heard the expression, "They are beside themselves with grief"? Soul loss is like that.

It's a feature, not a bug. It's normal and designed to protect the self that propels our body. The problem occurs when whatever tucked-away aspect of ourselves never returns. Because it was never safe for it to do so.

Sometimes we notice this absence quickly. Like, "I've really never been the same since my mom died." Sometimes it is more subtle—and is the build up of a million tiny cuts as we continue to curate a larger and larger shadow self.

Much of what Vedat Şar refers to as dissociative depression? It's a dispirited (dishilombished) self, because much of who you are has gone missing. This experience is also associated with anxiety, addiction, and autoimmune issues—all the stuff I talk about as trauma responses in my books.

And it's a vicious cycle: as we lose more and more parts of what enlivens us, we become even more susceptible to more loss at increasingly alarming rates.

The good news is that, throughout history, we as human beings have known that soul loss is real. And in traditional healing models, soul loss could be addressed through a process called soul retrieval. These traditional healing models are often referred to as shamanic models. Now, the word shaman comes from the Manchu-Tungus term *šaman*. *Sa* is a verb that means "to know." Therefore, a shaman is "one who knows." The term *shaman* didn't exist in any other Indigenous culture until the 1960s. For example, in Choctaw culture, we would reference our *alikchi* or *holkhunna*, but, over the years, the term *shaman* has become a pantraditional term, referencing anyone whose spirit is able to travel by means of altered states in order to assist one in healing. Shamans are the *ones who know*, after all. Unlike the word soul, the term *shaman* is a recognizable one that suits just fine, so we will continue to use it throughout.

Historically, soul retrieval is practiced with a shaman. It's a beautiful process, one I am not dismissing or diminishing at all. But it can also be a difficult service to access. Whether for expense, lack of availability, lack of support from your family—all that stuff. So the tools I am going to share with you for soul retrieval are designed to be self-directed.

And here's the thing: Soul retrieval work requires entering a space of non-ordinary reality. Meaning altering our own consciousness, which can sound scary, weird, or dangerous. Which makes sense, especially for those of us who already don't trust our brains terribly much. Until I had done more clinical training in various practices designed to alter our state of consciousness (e.g. hypnotherapy, brainspotting), I had the same concerns. But it turns out that all the research explicitly demonstrates that all this altered consciousness healing work is essentially self-created. In other words, your consciousness cannot be ethically altered without your consent. Therefore, gently leading yourself through the process is entirely doable.

Most of the research around altered states of consciousness has focused on subjective experiences, meaning what people noticed about themselves. In recent years, there has been more neuroscientific work around altered consciousness, starting with finding the neurological changes that take place in these experiences in order to better understand what individuals are explaining.

Put another way, altered consciousness is nothing more than a change from one's normal mental state. Therefore, it is relative, person to person. One of the best metaphors I heard for how it works was in my hypnotherapy coursework, where I was invited to consider the therapeutic approach as a door we open into this different state of consciousness, creating a safe container that allows the individuals we work with to access different aspects of themselves.

And the research we have about all this? Thus far, it demonstrates how complicated an internal process altering consciousness is. It's not just neurochemical but also metabolic. And it is something that can be induced by psychological means, not just as the result of medication, injury, and disease. We also know that, during states of altered consciousness, we as humans have an entirely different experience of sensory data, self-awareness, awareness of others, and even awareness of our own nervous system activation.

Fancy, fancy words to say: we have enormous and real capability to temporarily change how our bodies function. And those changes can allow us to do some deeper therapeutic work because we are more relaxed and focused while perceiving ourselves safe enough to process. One of my hypnotherapy trainers used the metaphor of opening a trap door into the deeper processes of the brain. We can get in and look at the stuff (shadow parts/lost soul parts/any other term that works well for you) we don't access during our daily lives.

So, in soul retrieval, we are engaging in a ritual of the mind, and using this work to create transformations within our lives. We are looking to go inward to connect more deeply with the pieces of ourselves that have been banished to the shadow.

Sometimes these parts return immediately, once recognized. Especially if we have done a lot of healing work already and they recognize it is safe to do so.

Sometimes there is more of a negotiation. Where we have to be patient with these parts, ask them what they need to feel safe to return, and do the work necessary to invite them home.

This is how we heal and restore our shilombish soul.

The Process, Defined

Based on the soul retrieval work of others, the work of anthropologists who studied soul retrieval across eras and cultures, and my own work in my practice, I've created a method for soul retrieval that can be self-lead or used with a healer or a healing community you already work with. Of course, do what resonates with you. If something feels weird or unwieldy or too activating? Adjust it, replace it, skip it, and see if you still get results you were looking for. If you don't? Then revisit and consider including the parts you are most worried about.

Here's an overview of the plan:

First, we bring in a deeper inspection of the shadow by completing a therapeutic deconstruction of our past and present relationships, to discern where the soul loss occurred. This is heavy work because it means looking at all the ways we have betrayed ourselves, both knowingly and unknowingly.

So how will we do this work in the pages to come? I promise, only a few more exercises! Here's what that will look like:

- Step 1: First, we are going to build on the shadow work we've already done with some deeper exploration into our individual circumstances. Your life doesn't look like mine, and mine doesn't look like yours right? And soul loss is so incredibly individual, not doing this first often leads to focusing on the wrong thing.

- Step 2: Create a personally meaningful ceremony to create space for a healing conversation with yourself. This may include music, lighting, and any items of comfort and care.

- Step 3: Breathwork. I know. I'm so sorry. But breathwork is incredibly helpful for creating a listening state within our bodies. I'm not going to guide you through one that is intentionally mind altering, like holotropic breathwork, because these techniques can be contraindicated with many medical conditions and are better done with guidance from a trained coach. You can use any other breathwork practices you already have a relationship with, but the diaphragmatic breathing exercise I'm including is a great one if you have less experience with breathwork. Diaphragmatic breathing (also known as belly breathing) causes a full oxygen exchange. That is, it uses your lungs to their fullest capacity, getting more oxygen into your system. This serves to lower your heart rate and blood pressure and increase both your relaxation and concentration abilities. All the stuff that is incredibly useful for accessing a deeper consciousness within ourselves.

- Step 4: A meditative practice where you look inward at your personal experience timeline, allowing you to find and care for these soul parts that have been lost to shame, including an inner dialogue where you honor the experiences of these parts (yourself!) and negotiate with them for wholeness and return.

Step 1: Deeper Exploration: Our History in Relation to Shame and Self-Criticism

Before we begin, it's important to consider our own personal histories when it comes to shame and its healing—through the lens of soul loss. The below exercise is designed to be introspective, reflexive work around your family of origin and other key individuals surrounding you growing up.

(Yes, I am totally trying to trick you into doing journaling work. But this is part of making the preconscious conscious, allowing us to open up to experiences that had become too painful with which to engage.)

Use these questions to reflect, whether in a physical journal or just for pondering as you go about your day (or days). You don't even have to do this in one sitting—whatever your process is.

- Growing up, who were the people you most counted on for your physical and emotional needs?

- Of these people, who had the biggest impact on your self-concept? This is often the person whose voice we internalize as our own as adults when we are beating ourselves up. The person who said,

"Don't eat that/don't say that/don't be like that" and other sundry recriminations.

- How did this main person most often demonstrate warmth and care?

- How did they respond to your distress? Your other complex emotions? Did you have any experiences of being soothed or having empathy expressed?

- Did you feel that they understood you and supported you? Not necessarily agreed with your outlook, but sat with your experience as valid.

- Or did they tell you your feelings were wrong/ needed to be changed?

- Or ignore your feelings?

- Or tease you about them, humiliating you further?

- Or did they generally display irritation/ displeasure?

- Or were their responses erratic, leaving you to not know what to expect in response?

- Were you neglected/bullied/abused? How so? (Broad strokes here—not great detail causing a bunch of activation of your nervous system right now . . . cuz this is hard enough.)

- Do you recall instances of humiliation? What do you remember? (Again broad strokes, looking for key incidents or patterns of responses.)

- What happened when your wants/needs/interests conflicted with theirs?

- Did they demonstrate excitement/support or irritation/anger when you misaligned with their expectations?

- What about other key people in your life?

- Other events that led to you feeling judged/devalued/degraded/humiliated/worthless/helpless?

Step 2: Personal Ceremony

The biggest reason I want to encourage you to create your own personalized healing ceremony is that I want it to have the deepest meaning for you as possible. If you and I were working together, me using my cultural practices with you would make sense because we are sharing an experience. But on your own? If I suggested all the tools I associate with ceremonial soul retrieval, without bringing my energy into the experience, it would seem interesting and exotic and intellectualized . . . *rather than a coming home to oneself.*

That sounded weird, so let me give you an example. A mestizo Mexicano client of mine also does smudges and cleansings as part of his emotional self-care. But in his family, they use romero (rosemary) instead of white sage. And where I seal with salt water, he uses agua de florida (florida water). Same ideas of cleansing and purification, different cultural attachments to how we do so.

And I know, my white friends reading right now might be feeling a little twitchy. Peoples who have become further removed from their own ancient cultural practices sometimes struggle even harder to find and connect to the ceremonial ways of their ancestors. But you have them, and there is so much available research now to help your journey.

If you don't have a lovely grandparent you can ask, start seeking the digital elders. Are you of Celtic descent? You may develop a strong relationship with yarrow and self-heal, for example.

Or, hell, it doesn't have to be that complicated. Maybe you connect strongly to the cedar that grew around your aunt's house growing up, and it's a smell you connect with love and safety because you often spent your summers with her.

This is all to say: ceremony has the deepest meaning and the strongest positive effects when it's personal.

And it all starts with figuring out how you want to feel while doing this work. Safe and cared for? Challenged and strengthened? What would that look like?

- What music would you associate with that feeling? Music that resonates with the human heartbeat (yes, I mean drumming) is commonly used, but maybe for you it's bagpipes? Electric guitar? You decide. It's also totally cool to listen to what's being marked as soul retrieval music if you have no idea where to start. Spotify, YouTube, etc. Listen and find what resonates with you.

- Location? Where do you most want to be that is reasonably accessible? I mean, I'd love to go travel to a mountaintop too, but that can take a lot of planning and resources, so what's available in your immediacy?

- What lighting? Natural sunlight? Candles? A fire pit? What most feels like home to you?

- What scents (herbs, oils, etc.)? We talked about burning herbs or candles, infusing your space with an olfactory experience that calls you home to yourself. What would they be?

- What about foods and drinks? Warm fresh bread? A cacao infused atole? Cool, fresh spring water? Maybe it's Mountain Dew in memory of your dad's favorite aunt who always made you feel safe and heard while she chugged them endlessly. Your ceremony—you decide.

- Clothing? What feels comfortable to wear? What helps you feel most connected? It may be a traditional cultural garment or your most comfortable old robe.

- Objects of importance? Maybe this is a special piece of jewelry? A picture of someone you love (maybe even a picture of YOU as a young child?), an instrument, a stone, a feather? What might you want to include?

After you build a meaningful ceremonial kit, then you can set aside your ceremonial time to start your soul retrieval work. But first up, the forewarned breathwork.

Step 3: Diaphragmatic Breathwork

When different forms of breathwork are compared, this form is the one that is most associated with altering our physiology in a way that is calming. Because researchers can't leave well enough alone, this form of breathwork is called cyclical sighing (because only the outbreath is through the mouth, I guess?), if you are interested in looking at some of the research itself. I've also heard it called belly breathing and tactical breathing. All the same thing.

The diaphragm is just a big ol' muscle that separates the chest cavity from the abdominal cavity. When we breathe from the diaphragm, we are breathing deeply enough to expand the abdomen instead of the chest, which slows our breathing process down—slowing the heart rate and decreasing our blood pressure.

On the inhale, the diaphragm contracts and presses on the abdominal organs, and on exhale, the diaphragm relaxes back against your spine. Fully exhaling is as important as fully inhaling because that's what creates space for the next deep inhale of fresh air, instead of mixing and recycling the old breath.

So, now that we've talked about *what* happens during diaphragmatic breathwork, here's the *how* to do it:

Lie down if you can. If you can't, relax your body the best you can without causing pain. Take care of you, no pretzeling unnecessarily. If you can lie comfortably, do so, keeping your knees bent and your feet hip-distance apart.

To help visualize the internal flow of your deep breaths, place one hand on your abdomen—which will rise and fall with your breaths—and the other hand on your chest.

Inhale through your nose, feeling your abdomen expand while your chest remains relatively still.

Pause, then slowly release your breath through your pursed lips, contracting your abdomen back down (again, something you will be able to feel under your hand).

Repeat, practicing for five to ten minutes.

And you don't have to use this technique just for shadow work or soul retrieval. You can practice this breathwork as a regular resource to help calm your vagal tone and have other health benefits. In fact, this practice will be easier to use with shadow work and soul retrieval if you are practicing with it regularly.

Step 4: Guided Meditation: A Journey through Time

As the next step in our soul retrieval journey, this meditative process explores your past and memories— through the lens of your relaxed nervous system. Here's the big trick though: we aren't going to try to steer into any specific memory. Interestingly, I've found that when using this technique with clients, we never go to the memory they expect/intend to go to. But where they did end up always makes complete sense.

You can use the recorded audio of this journey if the sound of my voice doesn't irritate the shit out of you. You can also record yourself reading it aloud, or have a loved one do the same.

If at any point this feels overly activating, that's entirely understandable. You can stop at any time, ok? You. Can. Stop. At. Any. Time. But if you feel you are getting somewhere and just need to defang the process a little bit, here are some things you can try:

- Change the memory images to black and white.
- Visualize a knob where you can turn down the sound or intensity.

- Put the memory up on a movie screen. Sit yourself in the theater and watch it from that vantage point. This creates a point of separation and space from the pain of the memory.

- Still too much? Put yourself up into the projection booth. Then you can look down at yourself, watching the screen. This creates two points of septaration from the pain of the memory.

I've used all of these memory-softening tricks in my practice, often more than one at a time. It's all about practice and finding what helps you process safely.

Guided Meditation Script

Our goal with this meditation is to explore times where you lost your sense of belonging in the world.

When you were young, you had an inherent sense of worth and value. You knew you were meant to be here. That your presence alone meant you deserve love and compassion. That you belong. That your existence is important.

As happens with most everyone at some point, something challenged that fundamental truth for you. Some incident or some person challenged your fundamental truth of belonging. Of deserving space in the world. You have lost sight of the truth that you are inherently deserving and that no one or no thing can take that from you.

Since that time, so many of your actions have revolved around you trying to re-earn your space. As if somehow you can gain it back through effort. You have spent more time achieving than being. Not for the joy of achievement or for creating good in the world, but as part of your payment for existence.

So when you have felt a sense of falling short in your payment plan, your punishment to yourself has been to withdraw. This hurts the people you love the most and it hurts you because you deprive yourself of connection, relationship, and support when you need it most.

The word *regression* is generally referred to as a return to something. A sense of going back. In this case, we are thinking even deeper than that. We are thinking like statisticians. In statistics, a regression equation allows us to predict future behavior, with small adjustments, based on past patterns. If we are able to go back to older points along the graph, we can see the pattern and readjust the equation. We can reclaim your future behavior. We can reclaim your sense of belonging in and to the world.

Take a moment to picture your own regression path in your mind. You can see many points along it that have deep meaning for you. Places that have influenced where you currently are.

I want you to choose one of those points for us to visit today. You are free to choose any point that makes the most sense to you right now. It doesn't have to be the furthest point on your line, or the closest. Just the one that your subconscious feels it is important to work on today.

What memory are you experiencing?

Who is there and how are they interacting with you?

What are you noticing?

What emotions and sensations are coming up?

Now, sit with that younger self, giving them space as they need it. Offer support and care. Start listening for the following information:

- What do you need to feel safe again?

- What do I need to commit to in order for you to come home?

•   •   •

It truly is ok if this takes a while. The idea of going on a soul retrieval and collecting all these parts and bringing them right home on the first try is pretty rare, even though those are the stories you will read about shamanic soul retrieval. In my experience, like everything else, it's a messy complicated process to heal. Because the original pain that caused the separation was also messy and complicated.

And even so, this journey is the fastest way through reconnecting with our lost aspects of self. Likely because it is one of (if not *the*) oldest healing practices humanity has. It is an innate healing experience that humans have had access to throughout history. Without the science of fMRIs and qEEGs and the like? We still understood that the human brain learns and processes through stories, and we sometimes can get to our deeper pain by working through these stories in an altered state.

CONCLUSION

*I*f this book was as hard to read as it was to write, we are both pretty exhausted right now. The more we dove into shame, the more complex and overwhelming and unsolvable it all seemed, didn't it?

But you hung in with me, as ready as I was for a different perspective and different path to healing.

And so, this is the TL;DR of what we covered:

Shame creates self-disgust and is often the product of how trauma disconnects us from our authentic selves. And modern treatments just aren't helping. To combat that vicious cycle, we looked at what causes the emotion of shame and how to use shadow work in our healing.

Then, we dove back further, into what our ancestors used to find their lost pieces of self and institute healing. Which gave us some new (ancient) tools to work with, in order to combat the idea of our fundamental brokenness, by calling home the aspects of ourselves that we had lost.

And yeah, that's hard work. But we've all done harder. Living as half-a-human because of dissociated trauma, hiding from yourself and those around you? Way harder.

You got this.

REFERENCES

Apps, M.A., Rushworth, M.F., & Chang, S.W. (2016). The Anterior Cingulate Gyrus and Social Cognition: Tracking the Motivation of Others. Neuron, 90(4), 692–707. doi.org/10.1016/j.neuron.2016.04.018.

Balban, M.Y., Neri, E., Kogon. M.M., Weed, L., Nouriani, B., Jo, B., Holl, G., Zeitzer, J.M., Spiegel, D., & Huberman, A.D. Brief structured respiration practices enhance mood and reduce physiological arousal. Cell Rep Med. 2023 Jan 17;4(1):100895. doi: 10.1016/j.xcrm.2022.100895. Epub 2023 Jan 10. PMID: 36630953; PMCID: PMC9873947.

Behavior Online (2000): A Conversation with Donald Nathanson.

Bértholo, J. (2017). Shadow working in project management: Understanding and addressing the irrational and unconscious in groups. Taylor & Francis.

Brink, N.E. (2013). The power of ecstatic trance: Practices for healing, spiritual growth, and accessing the universal mind. Bear & Co.

Budiarto, Y., & Helmi, A.F. (2021). Shame and Self-Esteem: A Meta-Analysis. Europe's journal of psychology, 17(2), 131–145. doi.org/10.5964/ejop.2115.

Buzekova, T. (2010). The shaman's journeys between emic and etic: representations of the shaman in neo-shamanism. Anthropological Journal of European Cultures, 19(1), 116+. link.gale.com/apps/doc/A396615467/AONE?u=oregon_oweb&sid=bookmark-AONE&xid=5f2126e0.

Bynum, W.E., 4th, Uijtdehaage, S., Artino, A.R., Jr, & Fox, J.W. (2020). The Psychology of Shame: A Resilience Seminar for Medical Students. MedEdPORTAL : the journal of teaching and learning resources, 16, 11052. doi.org/10.15766/mep_2374-8265.11052

Chappell, S., Cooper, E., & Trippe, G. (2019). Shadow work for leadership development. Journal of Management Development, 38(5), 326-335.

Chaplin, W.F., John, O.P., & Goldberg, L.R. (1988). Conceptions of states and traits: dimensional attributes with ideals as prototypes. Journal of personality and social psychology, 54(4), 541–557. doi.org/10.1037//0022-3514.54.4.541.

Chauhan, P., Rathawa, A., Jethwa, K., et al. The Anatomy of the Cerebral Cortex. In: Pluta R, editor. Cerebral Ischemia [Internet]. Brisbane (AU): Exon Publications; 2021 Nov 6. Chapter 1. Available from: ncbi.nlm.nih.gov/books/NBK575742/ doi: 10.36255/exonpublications.cerebralischemia.2021.cerebralcortex.

Children of the Code: The Compass of Shame (interview with Donald Nathanson)

Elison, J., Lennon, R., & Pulos, S. (2006). Investigating the compass of shame: The development of the Compass of Shame Scale. Social Behavior and Personality: An International Journal, 34(3), 221–238.

Elkins, D.N. (2022). Common Factors: What Are They and What Do They Mean for Humanistic Psychology? Journal of Humanistic Psychology, 62(1), 21–30. doi.org/10.1177/0022167819858533.

Fincham, G.W., Strauss, C., Montero-Marin, J., & Cavanagh, K. (2023). Effect of breathwork on stress and mental health: A meta-analysis of randomised-controlled trials. Scientific reports, 13(1), 432. doi.org/10.1038/s41598-022-27247-y.

Fishkin, G.L. (2016). The science of shame: And its treatment. Parkhurst Brothers Publishers Inc.

Goldman, B. (2020, September 16). Researchers pinpoint brain circuitry underlying dissociative experiences. med.stanford.edu/news/all-news/2020/09/researchers-pinpoint-brain-circuitry-underlying-dissociation.html.

Gore, B. (2001a). Ecstatic body postures: An alternative reality workbook (O). Bear & Company.

Guo, S. (2015). An investigation into the origin of the term "shaman". Sibirica: Interdisciplinary Journal of Siberian Studies, 14(3), 46+. link.gale.com/apps/doc/A447723408/AONE?u=oregon_oweb&sid=googleScholar&xid=09023a9f.

Hamasaki, H. Effects of Diaphragmatic Breathing on Health: A Narrative Review. Medicines (Basel). 2020 Oct 15;7(10):65. doi: 10.3390/medicines7100065. PMID: 33076360; PMCID: PMC7602530.

hooks, bell (2022). Teaching to transgress: Education as the practice of freedom. DEV Publishers & Distributors.

Iatrogenic and sociocognitive models of did. DID. (n.d.). did-research.org/controversy/iatrogenic

Ingerman, S. (2008). Soul retrieval: Mending the fragmented self. HarperOne, an imprint of HarperCollins Publishers.

Jeffrey., S. (2021, February 3). Shadow Work: A Complete Guide to Getting to Know Your Darker Half. scottjeffrey.com/shadow-work/.

Jette, C. (2000). Tarot Shadow Work: Using the Dark Symbols to Heal. Llewellyn Worldwide.

Jung, C.G. (1953). Psychology and alchemy. Routledge.

Jung, C.G., & Hull, R.F. (2008). On the nature of the psyche. Routledge.

Jung, C.G., & Pauli, W. (1955). The Interpretation of nature and the psyche.

Synchronicity: An acausal connecting principle. Pantheon Books.

Jung, C.G., & Read, H. (1976). Mysterium coniunctionis. Pantheon Books.

Kaufman, G. (1992). Shame: The power of caring. Schenkman Books.

Leeming, Dawn and Boyle, Mary (2004). Shame as a social phenomenon: A critical analysis of the concept of dispositional shame. Psychology and Psychotherapy:

Theory, Research & Practice, 77 (3). pp. 375-396. ISSN 1476-0835

Li, S., Wang, L. The effect of shame on prosocial behavior tendency toward a stranger. BMC Psychol 10, 308 (2022). doi.org/10.1186/s40359-022-01021-1.

Lighthorse, P., & Thompson, S. (2022). Goldmining the shadows: Honoring the medicine of wounds. Row House Publishing.

Linehan, M. (2015). DBT skills training handouts and worksheets. New York:The Guilford Press.

Loewenstein, R.J. (2018). Dissociation debates: everything you know is wrong. Dialogues in clinical neuroscience, 20(3), 229–242. doi.org/10.31887/DCNS.2018.20.3/rloewenstein

Luoma, J.B., Kohlenberg, B.S., Hayes, S.C., & Fletcher, L. (2012). Slow and steady wins the race: a randomized clinical trial of acceptance and commitment therapy targeting shame in substance use disorders. Journal of consulting and clinical psychology, 80(1), 43–53. doi.org/10.1037/a0026070.

Lyssenko, L., Schmahl, C., Bockhacker, L., Vonderlin, R., Bohus, M., & Kleindienst, N. (2018). Dissociation in psychiatric disorders: A meta-analysis of studies using the dissociative experiences scale. American Journal of Psychiatry, 175(1), 37–46. doi.org/10.1176/appi. ajp.2017.17010025.

Miller, T., & Nielsen, L. (2015). Measure of Significance of Holotropic Breathwork in the Development of Self-Awareness. Journal of alternative and complementary medicine (New York, N.Y.), 21(12), 796–803. doi. org/10.1089/acm.2014.0297.

Montagu, A. (1968). On being human. Hawthorn Books.

Morey, R. A., McCarthy, G., Selgrade, E.S., Seth, S., Nasser, J.D., & LaBar, K.S. (2012). Neural systems for guilt from actions affecting self versus others. NeuroImage, 60(1), 683–692. doi.org/10.1016/j.neuroimage.2011.12.069.

Murray, T. (2015). Contemplative Dialogue Practices: An inquiry into deep interiority, shadow work, and insight. Integral Leadership Review.

Peterson, A.L. (2022a, October 7). What is...the compass of shame. Mental Health @ Home. mentalhealthathome. org/2021/04/30/what-is-the-shame-compass/.

Porges, S.W. (2011). The polyvagal theory: Neurophysiological foundations of emotions, attachment, communication, and self-regulation. W.W. Norton.

Post-traumatic stress disorder (PTSD) and Complex PTSD. UK Trauma Council. (2023, November 29). uktraumacouncil.org/trauma/ptsd-and-complex-ptsd.

Rodriguez, L. M., Young, C. M., Neighbors, C., Tou, R., & Lu, Q. (2016). Cultural differences and shame in an expressive writing alcohol intervention. Journal of ethnicity in substance abuse, 15(3), 252–267. doi.org/10.10 80/15332640.2015.1024812.

Roth, G. (1998). Sweat your prayers: Movement as spiritual practice. Jeremy P. Tarcher/Putnam.

Salzberg, S., & Kabat-Zinn, J. (2020). Lovingkindness: The revolutionary art of happiness. Shambhala.

Şar, V. (2014). The many faces of dissociation: opportunities for innovative research in psychiatry. Clinical psychopharmacology and neuroscience : the official scientific journal of the Korean College of Neuropsychopharmacology, 12(3), 171–179. doi. org/10.9758/cpn.2014.12.3.171.

Şar, V., & Ozturk, E. (2014). Functional dissociation of the self: A sociocognitive approach to trauma and Dissociation. SSRN Electronic Journal. doi.org/10.2139/ ssrn.2462391.

Şar, V., Unal, S.N., & Ozturk, E. (2007). Frontal and occipital perfusion changes in dissociative identity disorder. Psychiatry research, 156(3), 217–223. doi.org/10.1016/j.pscychresns.2006.12.017.

Scheff, T.J. (2003). Shame in self and society. Symbolic Interaction, 26(2), 239–262. doi.org/10.1525/si.2003.26.2.239.

Sedighimornani, N. (2018). Shame and its features: understanding of shame. 10.5281/zenodo.1453426.

Self-compassionate letter (greater good in action). Greater Good In Action. (n.d.). ggia.berkeley.edu/practice/self_compassionate_letter.

Srinivasan, T.M. (2015). Healing altered states of consciousness. International journal of yoga, 8(2), 87–88. doi.org/10.4103/0973-6131.158468.

Soul healing: Unifying the lost part of yourself with your whole being. Kripalu. (2019). kripalu.org/resources/soul-healing-unifying-lost-part-yourself-your-whole-being.

Terrizzi Jr., J.A., & Shook, N. J. (2020a). On the Origin of Shame: Does Shame Emerge From an Evolved Disease-Avoidance Architecture?, Frontiers in Behavioral Neuroscience, 14. doi.org/10.3389/fnbeh.2020.00019.

The 6 human needs. Madanes Institute. (n.d.). madanesinstitute.com/the-6-human-needs/

Therapist resources: Compassion, shame, and self-criticism. ACT With Compassion. (n.d.). actwithcompassion.com/therapist_resources.

Tomkins, Silvan S. (1991), Affect Imagery Consciousness: Anger and Fear (Vol. 3). Springer.

Vitebsky, P. (1997, March). What is a shaman? Natural History, 106(2), 32+. link.gale.com/apps/doc/A19360545/AONE?u=oregon_oweb&sid=bookmark-AONE&xid=fc77dcfe

Wampold, B.E. (2001). The great psychotherapy debate: Models, methods and findings. Routledge.

Winnicott, D.W., Winnicott, C., Shepherd, R., & Davis, M. (2014). Home is where we start from: Essays by a Psychoanalyst. W.W. Norton & Company.

Yelsma, P., Brown, N.M., & Elison, J. (2002). Shame-focused coping styles and their associations with self-esteem. Psychological Reports, 90(3, part 2), 1179–1189.

APPENDIX A: POTENTIAL SOURCES OF A TRAUMA RESPONSE

*W*here does all that trauma come from? Here is a more inclusive, but still incomplete, list of common sources of trauma:

Child Abuse (physical, sexual, emotional, neglect): Child abuse is a huge category, and even the federal government has struggled to define it well. But essentially, any act (or failure to act/intervene) that harms a child or puts a child at imminent risk of harm is abuse. The younger the child, the more powerless and fragile they are, the more limitations there are to them being able to defend themselves or outcry, and the more risk there is for serious, ongoing abuse.

Domestic/Intimate Partner Violence (physical, sexual, emotional, economic, psychological): Domestic violence is the adult version of child abuse, for lack of a better comparison. It occurs in intimate partner/romantic relationships among both youth and adults. You do not have to be sharing a living space with your romantic partner for it to be considered domestic violence. The US Department of Justice notes a few differences in the types of violence that can occur in intimate partner relationships: Emotional abuse includes attacks on the partner's self-worth (e.g., criticism, name-calling). Psychological abuse is more action-oriented and can consist of isolating the partner, threatening harm to them or others that they care about, or destroying items that have meaning to them (without physically abusing them or other people). Economic abuse focuses on the way a partner creates a situation wherein they have all economic control in the relationship, forcing the abused partner to remain with them (controlling all money or not letting them have a job or get job training, for example).

Elderly/Disabled Adult Abuse (physical, sexual, emotional, neglect, exploitation): Unlike the above category, where the relationship is considered an equal one (until manipulated to be otherwise), some adults are considered by law to be powerless and fragile, and therefore have the same protections under the law that children are due. These individuals include older adults and individuals with physical or mental health impairments. The main difference between child abuse and elderly/disabled abuse is the concept of exploitation. An adult with income (for example, social security or retirement income) may have the use of that income exploited by another individual. While many adults have individuals who help them manage their money effectively—making sure their needs are met—there are many others who go without basics because that money is being mismanaged by their "caretaker."

Impaired Caregiver: Unlike in the above cases, caregivers who are not causing intentional harm or neglectful practices may still have their own impairments that make it difficult to render care, which can have a negative impact on the individuals they care for. For example, a child with a parent being treated for cancer may struggle with not having all their needs met due to the illness of the caretaker, coupled with the anxiety of seeing the illness and decline of the person who is their primary means of support and one of the people they love most in the world.

School Violence: School violence can consist of one-time, sentinel events (like a school shooting), or be the product of chronically dangerous school conditions (gang warfare, drug use, drug sales, fighting, etc.). If an individual is engaged in a school environment, and witnesses, partakes in, or is a victim of violence within it, that can be considered a traumatic event.

Community Violence: Living or working in certain communities can also pose a risk for trauma exposure. We can experience one-time, singular events (again, such as a shooting), or be exposed to violence on a regular basis by the nature of the common experiences found in the community to which we are exposed (drug use, fighting, etc.). Most community violence can be tied to neighborhoods that have been left impoverished of hope, opportunity, and money. Many of the other categories could also fall under the broad category of "community violence," but are widespread enough to merit their own section.

Bullying/Cyberbullying: Bullying is the use of one's strength or influence to control the actions of another. It can include real violence, the threat of violence, or intimidation to wield power over another. The traditional form of bullying is the older kid taking the lunch money of the younger one. But in the digital age, bullying can take many different forms. Electronic communication allows new ways of bullying to take place—from a distance and with anonymity in an increasing number of cases. This has allowed individuals who wouldn't normally have power over our lives to wreak serious havoc. Serious bullying experiences are often tied to a trauma response. Research I had done in my local community mental health agency demonstrated that an enormous portion of the children and youth that were brought to the mental health crisis center identified being bullied as the reason for their mental health crisis (often expressed in the form of suicidal or homicidal ideation). This reminded me at the time how incredibly important it is that we recognize the impact bullying can have on our emotional health and well-being.

Sexual Violence: Sexual violence often falls under the domain of child abuse or domestic partner violence. Other forms of sexual violence very well could fall under the heading of community violence. Sexual violence crosses all cultural and economic barriers.

Medical (illness or accident): Dealing with the negative impact of a health crisis (either a significant but short-term illness or a chronic condition) can be intensely traumatic. There's the loss of function and freedom from the health problem itself, and then there's the stress of accessing needed care and struggling to pay for it. Individuals with chronic, debilitating diseases which can be treated but not cured have to struggle with coming to terms with a "new normal," and many know that this disease will eventually no longer be treatable—and the decline accompanying that experience is terrifying.

Natural or Human-made Disasters: Natural disasters are events such as tornadoes, earthquakes, and floods that wreak havoc on our communities. Human-made disasters have a similar impact, but are the result of human action or inaction (such as industrial accidents like Chernobyl, Fukushima, or the Exxon Valdez spill). There can be significant overlap between the two, as failure in planning for or engaging in appropriate action during or after a natural disaster worsens the consequences, leaking into being a human-made disaster (i.e., studies of the Hurricane Katrina floods demonstrate that the majority of the flooding was due to faulty levees installed by the US Army Corps of Engineers, not the hurricane itself). This also relates to educating yourself about events that may have more extreme consequences for marginalized populations.

War/Terrorism: The standard definitions of these terms assume that war is engaged between willing participants with agreed-upon terms, while terrorism is conducted by renegades and targets innocent bystanders. Clearly, this isn't an accurate definition . . . however, the perception of one form of violence being more "acceptable" than the other has often led to a lack of understanding about the trauma inherent in both. While we expect and empathize with the suffering of the innocent bystander, the individuals who willingly serve as soldiers are also likely to struggle with PTSD or other trauma-related symptoms. According to the VA, 10 to 30% of soldiers have suffered PTSD sometime during their return home after being in a conflict (the statistics vary based on the service era). The US Department of Veterans Affairs released a statistic in 2013, citing approximately 22 veteran suicides occurring per day. No matter our role in such situations, the impact can be devastating. In addition, the military tends to consist of individuals who already belong to marginalized communities, who joined the military to escape poverty and who find themselves committing atrocities against those even poorer than themselves. (For example, Muhammad Ali's remark that no people of Vietnamese descent ever called him the N-word.)

Forced Displacement: We are sometimes forced to leave the only place we have known as home.

Oftentimes these reasons are for our own safety, but it can still be traumatic. It is important to remember that whether you are leaving war-torn Syria as a refugee or being placed in a foster home due to a parent's inability to provide adequate care, leaving your home and community is a trauma in and of itself. No matter how dire the circumstances are, being placed in new and unfamiliar surroundings and leaving the only home you have ever known requires a huge shift in thinking and behavior that is intensely difficult.

Traumatic Grief/Bereavement: While grief is a normal part of the human experience, some people struggle with intense loss in a similar way to other traumatic events, and they are unable to process the loss in a way that allows them to move forward.

Systems Trauma: Individuals who are subject to some sort of system are also at risk for trauma response. For example, children in foster care or the juvenile justice system may struggle with the trauma associated with the events that resulted in their entering the system, the trauma of the displacement experience, and then the continued trauma of having very little power and control over their experience within the system. Not knowing what your future will look like, being unable to form support networks due to continued movement and staff turnover, and not being able to obtain accurate information about your situation are all common experiences. A system itself often perpetuates its own ongoing form of trauma that cannot be discounted when we look at the experiences that shape us.

Intergenerational Trauma: Historical oppression and its consequences are often transmitted down generations. This can happen through continued poverty and lack of opportunity in communities (such as Indian reservations), as well as within our literal genetic code. Trauma experienced by our parents and grandparents has the capacity to change our epigenetic structure in utero, causing many individuals to be born with a hardwired trauma response.

In summary, these are just some of the things that can be a trauma. In the end, we all experience trauma differently and are impacted by too many things to list. Creating a list that touches only on the big "diagnosable" categories dismisses other experiences that shouldn't be dismissed.

So this list is intended to start conversations, and maybe help you realize the legitimacy of some life experiences as being traumatic. And while my list is more inclusive than one you will read in the DSM, it still may not fit your circumstances. And also? Trauma doesn't operate by checking the right box in the right category. So I hope that you will believe me when I say your experiences and reactions are valid and real and you are worthy of care and the opportunity to heal.

APPENDIX B: TIPS FOR PRACTITIONERS

For those of you in helping professions looking at incorporating what we've discussed in this book into your work, here are some resources that may help your practice:

Trainings

- Breathwork: various modalities and trainers, such as . . .

    ○ medical breathwork

    ○ yogic breathwork (pranayama)

    ○ holotropic breathwork (NOTE: For safety, please be VERY well trained in this if you are using it!)

- Brainspotting (David Grand)

- Somatic Archeology (Ruby Gibson, Freedom Lodge)
- Hypnotherapy (various modalities and trainers)
- Trauma-Informed Care (various modalities and trainers)
- Adverse Childhood Experiences
    ○ The state of California ACESAware training is available for free, even if you are not licensed/working in the state of California
- Movement Training (trauma-informed yoga, dance, Tai Chi, Qi Gong, etc.)

Books

- *Soul Retrieval: Mending The Fragmented Self* by Sandra Ingerman
- *Gold Mining the Shadows* by Pixie Lighthorse
- *The Power of Ecstatic Trance: Practices for Healing, Spiritual Growth, and Accessing the Universal Mind* by Nicholas E. Brink
- *Ecstatic Body Postures: An Alternate Reality Workbook* by Belinda Gore

- *Sweat Your Prayers: The Five Rhythms of the Soul* by Gabrielle Roth

ABOUT THE AUTHOR

Dr. Faith G. Harper, ACS, ACN, holds postdoctoral certifications in sexology and applied clinical nutrition and is trained in yoga, meditation, breathwork, mindful movement, and all of those other forms of care that make most people avoid her at parties. In the past, she has worked in academia, community mental health, and private practice as a licensed professional counselor. She maintains a connection with academia through her work with the Society of Indian Psychologists. She lives in San Antonio, TX, with her amazing friends and family and terrible rescue cats. She can be reached through her website, faithgharper. com.

MORE BY DR. FAITH

Books

The Autism Partner Handbook (with Joe Biel and Elly Blue)

The Autism Relationships Handbook (with Joe Biel)

Befriend Your Brain

Coping Skills

How to Be Accountable (with Joe Biel)

This Is Your Brain on Depression

Unfuck Your Addiction

Unfuck Your Adulting

Unfuck Your Anger

Unfuck Your Anxiety

Unfuck Your Blow Jobs

Unfuck Your Body

Unfuck Your Boundaries

Unfuck Your Brain

Unfuck Your Cunnilingus

Unfuck Your Friendships

Unfuck Your Grief

Unfuck Your Intimacy

Unfuck Your Kink

Unfuck Your Stress

Unfuck Your Worth

Unfuck Your Writing (with Joe Biel)

Woke Parenting (with Bonnie Scott)

Workbooks

Achieve Your Goals

The Autism Relationships Workbook (with Joe Biel)

How to Be Accountable Workbook (with Joe Biel)

Unfuck Your Anger Workbook

Unfuck Your Anxiety Workbook

Unfuck Your Body Workbook

Unfuck Your Boundaries Workbook

Unfuck Your Intimacy Workbook

Unfuck Your Worth Workbook

Unfuck Your Year

Zines

The Autism Handbook (with Joe Biel)

BDSM FAQ

Defriending

Detox Your Masculinity (with Aaron Sapp)

Emotional Freedom Technique

Getting Over It

How to Find a Therapist

How to Say No

Indigenous Noms

Relationshipping

The Revolution Won't Forget the Holidays
Self-Compassion
Sex Tools
Sexing Yourself
STI FAQ (with Aaron Sapp)
Surviving
This Is Your Brain on Addiction
This Is Your Brain on Grief
This Is Your Brain on PTSD
Unfuck Your Consent
Unfuck Your Dating
Unfuck Your Forgiveness
Unfuck Your Mental Health Paradigm
Unfuck Your Parenting #1–6 (with Bonnie Scott)
Unfuck Your Sleep
Unfuck Your Work
Vision Boarding

Other

Boundaries Conversation Deck
Intimacy Conversation Deck
Stress Coping Skills Deck
How Do You Feel Today? (poster)

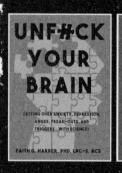

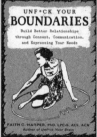